Hate Crimes

Hate Crimes

Other Books in the Current Controversies Series:

Hate Crimes

Tamara L. Roleff, *Book Editor*

David Bender, *Publisher*
Bruno Leone, *Executive Editor*

Bonnie Szumski, *Editorial Director*
Stuart B. Miller, *Managing Editor*

CURRENT CONTROVERSIES

Cover photo: © Reuters/CORBIS

Library of Congress Cataloging-in-Publication Data

Hate crimes / Tamara L. Roleff, book editor.
    p. cm. — (Current controversies)
    Includes bibliographical references and index.
    ISBN 0-7377-0453-5 (pbk. : alk. paper) — ISBN 0-7377-0454-3 (lib. bdg. : alk. paper)
    1. Hate crimes—United States. I. Roleff, Tamara L. II. Series.

HV6773.52 .H365   2001
364.1—dc21
                        00-037205
                        CIP

©2001 by Greenhaven Press, Inc., PO Box 289009, San Diego, CA 92198-9009
Printed in the U.S.A.

Contents

Chapter 2: Should Hate Speech Be Restricted?

Yes: Hate Speech Should Be Restricted

No: Hate Speech Should Not Be Restricted

Chapter 3: Are Federal Hate Crime Laws Necessary?

Yes: Federal Hate Crime Laws Are Necessary

No: Federal Hate Crime Laws Are Unnecessary

Chapter 4: Which Groups Pose a Threat to Society?

Foreword

By definition, controversies are "discussions of questions in which opposing opinions clash" (Webster's Twentieth Century Dictionary Unabridged). Few would deny that controversies are a pervasive part of the human condition and exist on virtually every level of human enterprise. Controversies transpire between individuals and among groups, within nations and between nations. Controversies supply the grist necessary for progress by providing challenges and challengers to the status quo. They also create atmospheres where strife and warfare can flourish. A world without controversies would be a peaceful world; but it also would be, by and large, static and prosaic.

The Series' Purpose

The purpose of the Current Controversies series is to explore many of the social, political, and economic controversies dominating the national and international scenes today. Titles selected for inclusion in the series are highly focused and specific. For example, from the larger category of criminal justice, Current Controversies deals with specific topics such as police brutality, gun control, white collar crime, and others. The debates in Current Controversies also are presented in a useful, timeless fashion. Articles and book excerpts included in each title are selected if they contribute valuable, long-range ideas to the overall debate. And wherever possible, current information is enhanced with historical documents and other relevant materials. Thus, while individual titles are current in focus, every effort is made to ensure that they will not become quickly outdated. Books in the Current Controversies series will remain important resources for librarians, teachers, and students for many years.

In addition to keeping the titles focused and specific, great care is taken in the editorial format of each book in the series. Book introductions and chapter prefaces are offered to provide background material for readers. Chapters are organized around several key questions that are answered with diverse opinions representing all points on the political spectrum. Materials in each chapter include opinions in which authors clearly disagree as well as alternative opinions in which authors may agree on a broader issue but disagree on the possible solutions. In this way, the content of each volume in Current Controversies mirrors the mosaic of opinions encountered in society. Readers will quickly realize that there are many viable answers to these complex issues. By questioning each author's conclusions, students and casual readers can begin to develop the critical thinking skills so important to evaluating opinionated material.

Current Controversies is also ideal for controlled research. Each anthology in the series is composed of primary sources taken from a wide gamut of informational categories including periodicals, newspapers, books, United States and foreign government documents, and the publications of private and public organizations. Readers will find factual support for reports, debates, and research papers covering all areas of important issues. In addition, an annotated table of contents, an index, a book and periodical bibliography, and a list of organizations to contact are included in each book to expedite further research.

Perhaps more than ever before in history, people are confronted with diverse and contradictory information. During the Persian Gulf War, for example, the public was not only treated to minute-to-minute coverage of the war, it was also inundated with critiques of the coverage and countless analyses of the factors motivating U.S. involvement. Being able to sort through the plethora of opinions accompanying today's major issues, and to draw one's own conclusions, can be a complicated and frustrating struggle. It is the editors' hope that Current Controversies will help readers with this struggle.

Greenhaven Press anthologies primarily consist of previously published material taken from a variety of sources, including periodicals, books, scholarly journals, newspapers, government documents, and position papers from private and public organizations. These original sources are often edited for length and to ensure their accessibility for a young adult audience. The anthology editors also change the original titles of these works in order to clearly present the main thesis of each viewpoint and to explicitly indicate the opinion presented in the viewpoint. These alterations are made in consideration of both the reading and comprehension levels of a young adult audience. Every effort is made to ensure that Greenhaven Press accurately reflects the original intent of the authors included in this anthology.

"The need for and legitimacy of stiffer sentences for crimes that are based on prejudice and the victim's identity are at the heart of Americans' concerns about hate crimes."

Introduction

Two bicyclists were riding down a country road in Wyoming in early October 1998 when they noticed what appeared to be a scarecrow tied spread-eagle to a split-rail fence. Upon further investigation, they discovered that the scarecrow was actually a young man who had been so badly beaten that he was in a coma. The man was Matthew Shepard, a gay student at the University of Wyoming in Laramie. The night before, Shepard had been in a bar where he tried to pick up two men, Russell Henderson and Aaron McKinney. The two lured Shepard out to their truck by pretending to be gay, then robbed him of $20, pistol-whipped him, and lashed him to the fence, where he remained in near-freezing temperatures for almost eighteen hours before his discovery. Four days later, Shepard died, never awakening from his coma.

Shepard's murder was immediately branded a "hate crime" by gay activists and those who monitor such crimes. A hate crime is generally understood to mean a crime against a victim who is chosen specifically because of his or her race, religion, gender, national origin, disability, and in some states, sexual orientation. While "hate crime" is a relatively new addition to legal terminology, appearing about the mid-1980s, it is not a new concept. According to James B. Jacobs and Kimberly Potter, authors of *Hate Crimes: Criminal Law and Identity Politics*, American history has seen many notorious incidents of anti-Semitic, anti-Catholic, xenophobic, homophobic, and antiblack violence. However, Americans have been increasingly less accepting of bigotry since the civil rights era of the 1960s, and hence, the emergence and acceptance of the distinct category of "hate crime."

In 1990 Congress passed the Hate Crime Statistics Act, which required the Department of Justice to collect and publish statistics about crimes that were bias-related. As a result, reporting of such crimes increased dramatically. An index of newspapers showed that only eleven articles about hate crimes were published in 1985. In 1990, there were 511 references to hate crimes, and that number doubled in 1993. With increased recognition of hate crimes, minority advocates began fighting for penalty enhancement laws for these crimes. Penalty enhancement laws allow judges to increase the sentence of a criminal convicted of a crime committed because of the victim's race, gender, nationality, religion, or sexual orientation.

Hate Crimes

Shepard's murder heightened the controversy over hate crime laws. Wyoming, where Shepard was murdered, has no such laws. Moreover, many states do not include sexual orientation as a protected class in their hate crime laws. Supporters of hate crime legislation contend that these laws are necessary to reinforce society's message that prejudice and hate are unacceptable and to deter hate crimes. Sociologists Jack Levin and Jack McDevitt assert in their book *Hate Crimes: The Rising Tide of Bigotry and Bloodshed*,

> A strong prison sentence sends a signal to would be hatemongers everywhere that should they illegally express their bigotry, they can expect to receive more than a mere slap on the wrist.

Penalty enhancement laws for hate crimes are necessary, they claim, because crimes committed because of bias or hate are more morally reprehensible than other crimes.

Other supporters of such legislation maintain that perpetrators of hate crimes are trying to send a message of intimidation to whatever group is being targeted. Senators Edward Kennedy and Arlen Specter, sponsors of a federal hate-crime bill that has yet to pass in Congress, explain, "Hate crimes are uniquely destructive and divisive because they injure not only the immediate victim but the community and sometimes the nation." For example, they maintain that the hate crime committed against Shepard tells gays in Laramie, in Wyoming, and across the United States that gays are still the objects of prejudice and hate, and that they can never feel safe because any one of them might be the next victim.

Hate crime legislation supporters also contend that hate crimes cause the victims more physical and psychological harm than other types of crimes and so the punishment should be greater. According to law professors Bennett Weisburd and Brian Levin, "Because the violence is so brutal, the degradation so complete and the vulnerability so omnipresent, bias crime victims exhibit greater psychological trauma than nonbias victims."

Others argue, however, that penalty enhancement laws for hate crimes are unnecessary and will do little to prevent hate crimes. They point out that all the offenses covered under hate crime laws are already prosecutable crimes and that additional penalties would not be effective. According to the editors of the *New Republic*, even if Wyoming had had a hate crime law in effect at the time of Shepard's murder, it would not have saved his life:

> [Hate crime laws] would probably have little effect on the occurrence of hate crimes against gays. It's hard to see how Matthew Shepard's killers would have been deterred by the prospect of federally assisted prosecution and a tough federal penalty. Under Wyoming law, and that of most states, murder is already punishable by the ultimate penalty: death.

Henderson and McKinney managed to narrowly avoid the death penalty by agreeing to a last-minute plea bargain during their trial; they were each sentenced to two consecutive life sentences with no possibility of parole.

Introduction

Some opponents to hate crime laws object to increasing an offender's sentence due to the alleged motive of the crime. They cite two constitutional amendments for their opposition: equal protection and free speech. Protecting certain groups because of their identity will eventually threaten Americans' right to free speech, they assert. The editors of the *New Republic* argue:

> The basic problem with which all proposed hate-crime laws must contend is that they create a legal distinction between someone who kills a gay man because he hates gays and someone who kills a gas-station attendant in order to steal from his cash register. To create such a distinction in effect penalizes some criminals more harshly, not because of their deeds, but because of their beliefs. This clashes with constitutional principles protecting free thought and equality under the law.

Instead of adding mandatory penalty enhancements to laws, opponents maintain that judges should be given more latitude when sentencing criminals. They contend that judges must be given the discretion to factor in the criminal's motives for and the circumstances surrounding the crime when determining the sentence.

The need for and legitimacy of stiffer sentences for crimes that are based on prejudice and the victim's identity are at the heart of Americans' concerns about hate crimes. *Hate Crimes: Current Controversies* explores this topic as well as the extent and seriousness of hate crimes, whether hate speech should be protected under the First Amendment, and whether certain groups incite hate and violence.

Legal philosopher Jeffrie Murphy explains, "All assaults, whether racial or not, involve motives of humiliation and are thus evil to the same degree." Others argue that hate crimes are not more brutal than other crimes in the same category; if they were, then they would be categorized as a more brutal crime—for example, aggravated assault rather than simple assault. Jacobs and Potter also maintain that using victims' psychological trauma as a justification for passing hate crime legislation is misguided. "It should come as no surprise that hate crime victims report psychological and emotional effects. *All victims do*," they assert.

Chapter 1

Are Hate Crimes a Serious Problem?

Overview: What Is a Hate Crime?

by James B. Jacobs and Kimberly Potter

About the authors: *James B. Jacobs is the director of New York University's Center for Research in Crime and Justice and a law professor at the NYU School of Law. Kimberly Potter, a former senior research fellow at NYU's Center for Research in Crime and Justice, is a lawyer in private practice in New York. They are the authors of* Hate Crimes: Criminal Law and Identity Politics.

> [C]rimes motivated by bigotry usually arise not out of the pathological rantings and ravings of a few deviant types in organized hate groups, but out of the very mainstream of society.
>
> Jack Levin and Jack McDevitt, *Hate Crimes:*
> *The Rising Tide of Bigotry and Bloodshed*

We cannot talk about how much hate crime exists in the United States or what to do about it until we are clear about what a hate crime is. This viewpoint shows that the concept of hate crime is loaded with ambiguity because of the difficulty of determining (1) what is meant by prejudice; (2) which prejudices qualify for inclusion under the hate crime umbrella; (3) which crimes, when attributable to prejudice, become hate crimes; and (4) how strong the causal link must be between the perpetrator's prejudice and the perpetrator's criminal conduct.

Complexity of Prejudice

"Hate" crime is not really about hate, but about bias or prejudice. Statutory definitions of hate crime differ somewhat from state to state, but essentially hate crime refers to criminal conduct motivated by prejudice. Prejudice, however, is a complicated, broad, and cloudy concept. We all have prejudices for and against individuals, groups, foods, countries, weather, and so forth. Sometimes these prejudices are rooted in experience, sometimes in fantasy and irrationality, and sometimes they are passed down to us by family, friends, school, religion, and culture. Some prejudices (e.g., anti-Fascist) are considered good, some (e.g., preference for tall people over short people) relatively innocuous; but other prejudices provoke strong social and political censure (e.g., racism, anti-Semitism, misogyny). Even in this latter group there is a great deal of confusion about what constitutes an acceptable opinion or preference (e.g., "I prefer to attend a historically black college," or "I oppose Zionism and a Jewish state," or "I don't like men as much as women") and what constitutes unacceptable, abhorrent prejudice.

Though sociologists and social psychologists have long wrestled with the concept of prejudice, they have been unable to agree on a single definition. One point of consensus is that

> *"'Hate' crime is not really about hate, but about bias or prejudice."*

there are many kinds of prejudice. An individual can be prejudiced in favor of something (e.g., his religion) or prejudiced against something (e.g., someone else's religion). . . .

Often groups and individuals reject the accusation that they are prejudiced or argue that their prejudices are justified because they amount to factually correct observations. For example, some white "separatists" and even white supremacists characterize themselves not as anti-black, but as pro-white. (One segment of the Afrikaner population in South Africa advocates a homeland for Afrikaners to preserve Afrikaner language and culture and insists that this is not an expression of racism toward blacks.) A white person who is persuaded by the evidence presented in Charles Murray's and Richard Herenstein's controversial book, *The Bell Curve,* that the mean IQ of blacks is lower than the mean IQ of whites might object to being labeled a racist. Likewise, some blacks in the United States insist that Afro-centrism is not (or, at least, is not necessarily) an expression of anti-white prejudice. Resolving these claims, especially with respect to particular groups and situations, is no easy matter.

The apparent ease with which individuals develop prejudice has no single explanation. Professor and Harvard psychologist Gordon Allport noted in his book, *The Nature of Prejudice,* that "[t]he easiest idea to sell anyone is that he is better than someone else." Accordingly, most prejudices have some "functional significance" for the individual—they make the individual feel secure, provide a source of self-esteem, or explain social or economic problems (i.e., scapegoating). For some individuals, prejudice may simply be "a matter of blind conformity with prevailing folkways." In other words, a person may grow up *assuming* that members of another group are mean, stingy, dirty, weak, stupid, or inferior, because that is what she has always been told. Hatred may not be involved at all; indeed, some individuals holding such views may view themselves as well-intentioned paternalists. . . .

Whether a particular individual or even a particular opinion should be counted as prejudiced is sometimes debatable. For example, is a cab driver who fears picking up young black males in New York City prejudiced, when young black males commit the majority of taxi robberies? Some people argue that supporters of caps on welfare benefits and those who question the wisdom of affirmative action are racists. Sometimes an individual need not say or do anything to warrant being labeled "prejudiced." For example, a women's studies professor at Brandeis University, Becky Thompson, explained that her teaching methods begin with the premise that "it is not open to debate whether a white student is racist or a male student is sexist. He/she simply is." The word "prejudice" is often used so loosely that it can characterize the values, beliefs, and attitudes of most Americans.

Consider this example. The National Conference (formerly the National Conference of Christians and Jews) found that 55 percent of a survey's respondents believe that Catholics "want to impose their own ideas of morality on the larger society." The National Conference concluded that this was proof of widespread anti-Catholic prejudice. A critic might object that the survey respondents were giving an accurate response based upon their perception that Catholics, or at least the Catholic Church, had strong feelings and positions on matters on the social agenda like abortion, homosexuality, government aid to parochial schools, and assisted suicide.

If practically everyone holds some prejudiced values, beliefs, and attitudes, every crime by a member of one group against a member of another group might be a hate crime; at least it ought to be investigated as such. Moreover, since criminals, as a

> *"Whether a particular individual or even a particular opinion should be counted as prejudiced is sometimes debatable."*

group, are surely less tolerant and respectful of others than noncriminals, they are disproportionately likely to be motivated by prejudice. Indeed, in one sense, all (or at least most) violent crimes could be attributed, at least in part, to the offender's prejudice against the victim, based upon the victim's race, gender, age, size, looks, perceived wealth, perceived attitude, and so forth.

Which Prejudices Transform Crime into Hate Crime?

Criminals probably have many conscious and unconscious prejudices, for example, against people who are (or appear to be) rich, poor, successful, unsuccessful, drunks, drug addicts, and so forth. These prejudices are not politically salient in contemporary American society, and would not, even if they are motivating factors, transform ordinary crime into hate crime. By contrast, racial, religious, and gender prejudices are widely and vigorously condemned. These prejudices are officially denounced in our laws and political discourse. Hate crime laws constitute a "next generation" effort. They condemn these traditionally and officially designated prejudices when they are held by and acted upon by criminals. By "officially designated prejudices," we mean to highlight that not all abhorrent prejudices are chosen by the federal and state legislatures for official censure. The legislatures choose which prejudices they want to officially condemn. In some states, sexual orientation bias is included in the hate crime laws, in other states it is not. The same goes for gender bias, bias based upon mental or physical disability, and bias based on age.

The civil rights paradigm that has condemned and outlawed certain prejudices in employment and housing does not apply easily to the world of crime. The first problem is that some of the groups that are the classic targets of prejudice serve as active perpetrators of prejudice-motivated crime. It is true that anti-discrimination laws protect white job applicants from being discriminated against by black employers, but that scenario rarely arises and, for that reason, does not have to be dealt with in considering the desirability of anti-discrimination legislation. Many commentators continue to portray the United States as a nation of two races, a dominant and oppressive white race and a subjugated and victimized black race. That picture, while a caricature, is more accurate in the context of employment and housing than with respect to crime. The majority of crimes are intraracial (i.e., the perpetrator and victim are members of the same racial group). Eighty percent of violent crimes involve an offender and victim of the same race. Ninety-two percent of black murder victims and 66.6 percent of white murder victims are killed by murderers of the same race. For the 20 percent of violent crimes that are interracial, 15 percent involve black offenders and white victims; 2 percent involve white offenders and black victims; and 3 percent involve other combinations. Robbery is the crime with the highest interracial percentage; 37 percent involve victims and offenders of different races: 31 percent involve black offenders and white victims, 4 percent involve other-race offenders and white victims, and just 2 percent involve white offenders and nonwhite victims.

Black Offender/White Victim

The number of black offender/white victim crimes has made some strong proponents of hate crime laws uncomfortable. Some argue that black offenders who attack white victims are motivated by economics not prejudice. A few have proposed removing crimes based upon anti-white prejudice from the definition of hate crime. After the shootings (black perpetrator, white victims) and arson at Freddy's clothing store in Harlem in 1995, which resulted in the death of eight people, a number of politicians argued that the crime should not be seen as a

> *"If practically everyone holds some prejudiced values, beliefs, and attitudes, every crime by a member of one group against a member of another group might be a hate crime."*

racial incident, but rather as a business dispute over a lease between the owner of Freddy's, who was Jewish and the owner of the adjacent store, who was black. The crime was committed by a black man, who previously had participated in demonstrations outside Freddy's that involved racial insults against customers, and threats against the owner and employees.

Jill Tregor, executive director of San Francisco's Intergroup Clearinghouse, which provides legal services and counseling to hate crime victims, claims that white crime victims are using hate crime laws to enhance penalties against minorities, who already experience prejudice within the criminal justice system.

> *"Racial, religious, and gender prejudices are widely and vigorously condemned."*

One law review author proposes that in cases of interracial assault by a white offender, *prejudice should be presumed*, and the burden placed on the defendant to prove the absence of a prejudiced motivation. No such presumption would apply in interracial attacks by black perpetrators.

In theory, it would be possible to exclude from the definition of hate crime those crimes motivated by minority group members' prejudice against whites on the ground that such prejudices are more justified or understandable, and the crimes less culpable, or less destructive to the body politic than crimes by whites against minorities. But such an argument would be difficult to construct, and might well violate the Fourteenth Amendment's Equal Protection Clause.

Just as it makes no sense to presume the prejudice of white offenders against black victims, it makes little sense to argue that black offenders cannot ever be prejudiced against their white victims. Black prejudice and even hatred of whites, and especially Jews, is well documented. When the Reverend Louis Farrakhan, Nation of Islam leader, mentioned Colin Ferguson, the Long Island Railroad mass murderer, at a rally in New York City, the audience cheered. In a speech before an audience of 2,000 at Howard University, Nation of Islam spokesman Khalid Muhammad drew loud applause when he stated, "I love Colin Ferguson, who killed all those white folks on the Long Island train." Louis Farrakhan is probably the best-known avowedly racist and anti-Semitic black leader, but examples of such prejudice are common in the black press and radio, at least in the New York City area. On April 19, 1989, a white female jogger was beaten and gang-raped by a group of black youths. After months of rehabilitation, she still suffered from vision, balance, and olfactory problems. Attorney Alton Maddox, Jr., during a program on black radio station WLIB, claimed that the gang rape of the "Central Park jogger" was a racist hoax and questioned whether the victim had really been hurt. "Who," he asked, "had seen the victim before her suspiciously 'miraculous recovery?'" The *Amsterdam News,* a black newspaper, published the victim's name and labeled the prosecution a racist conspiracy.

A second problem in importing the basic civil rights paradigm from the employment and housing contexts to the crime context is the sheer pervasiveness of prejudice, of one type or another, that plays a role of some kind in a large percentage of crimes. Because of that pervasiveness it will be difficult to prevent the category of hate crime, if defined broadly, from expanding to be coextensive with the entire criminal law.

Our basic civil rights paradigm does not deal extensively with prejudice among European ethnic groups. However, such prejudices are a salient feature of American history and still are apparent in some criminality. Should the criminal law and the criminal justice apparatus begin hunting out these prejudices in "white-on-white" personal and property crimes?

Perhaps some percentage of black-on-black, Hispanic-on-Hispanic, and Asian-on-Asian crime could also be attributed to prejudice if we scour every crime for evidence. The contemporary multicultural discourse refers to "Hispanics," "Asians," and "Africans" as if they were single homogeneous groups without divisive ethnicities. Only a moment's reflection is needed to dispel that misconception. These classifications disguise enormous differences, historic animosities, and prejudices.

Racial Prejudices

Asian-American is perhaps the most distortive term. Asia, the world's largest continent, includes nationality, ethnic, tribal, and religious groups whose prejudices against one another are every bit as palpable as European ethnic prejudices. Consider the animosities between Sunni Muslims and Shiite Muslims and between Muslims and Hindus, between Muslims and Sikhs, and between Pakistanis and Indians. Consider the animosities and hatreds between Chinese and Tibetans, between Japanese and Chinese, and between Koreans and Japanese. There are intense, centuries-old hatreds held in Vietnam by minority ethnic groups against the majority and in Cambodia by the Khem against the Vietnamese minority. Therefore, if hate crime is to become a basic category for defining crime, it will be necessary to get beyond thinking of "Asians" as a homogeneous group among whose members only nonhate crimes exist. Once we begin hunting down prejudices in criminals' motivations, we will find them in abundance.

> *"These classifications [of 'Hispanics,' 'Asians,' and 'Africans' as single homogeneous groups] disguise enormous differences, historic animosities, and prejudices."*

Since the late 1980s, there has been an increasing amount of attention to the nationality and ethnic differences masked by the blanket term "Hispanic." But anyone familiar with Latin America and the Caribbean Islands knows that there are great differences among the peoples and cultures of this area. Just as European nationality groups have their own cultures, foods, myths, and histories, so too do Argentineans, Colombians, Cubans, Mexicans, Nicaraguans, Puerto Ricans, and so forth. There is no reason to exclude prejudices among and between these peoples from the hate crime concept.

Sub-Sahara Africa is plagued by ethnic and tribal hatreds. Only recently, the world has been appalled by massacres of the Tutsis and Hutus in Rwanda, the Ibo and Hausa in Nigeria, and the Zulu and Xhosa in South Africa. If members of these groups immigrate to the United States and commit crimes against one another, we will have yet another potential species of hate crime. Even the category "African American" disguises ethnic or national prejudices, for example, between American blacks and blacks of Caribbean descent. Intrablack prejudice also extends to what is called, "colorism," or prejudice based on the darkness or lightness of skin color. Are all of these ethnic or color prejudices the proper subject of hate crime laws? If not, what principle enables us to impose extra punishments for offenders who act out only certain prejudices, but not others?

Sexism

The women's movement emerged as a political force later than the black civil rights movement, but today it is equally well entrenched. Sexism is widely seen as racism's counterpart, and denunciations of racism and sexism are frequently uttered in the same breath. Thus, as a matter of first impression, it would be natural to include gender prejudice under the hate crime umbrella, especially in light of the extent to which women as a group are victimized by men. Indeed, crimes against women would seem to be the most obvious candidate for recognition as hate crime. For women, crime is overwhelmingly an intergroup phenomenon. In 1994, women reported approximately 500,000 rapes and sexual assaults, almost 500,000 robberies and 3.8 million assaults. The perpetrator was male in the vast majority of these offenses.

There is every reason to believe that a high percentage of male violence against women is motivated, at least in part, by anti-female prejudice, especially if prejudice is broadly defined. Practically every act of male violence and intimidation against women is a potential hate crime. Should all crimes by men against women be counted twice, first as generic crimes (murder, assault, rape) and second as hate crimes? And should every crime by a male against a female receive a harsher penalty than the same crime when committed by a male against a male? Surprisingly, there has been strong political resistance to treating crimes by men against women as hate crimes.

"There has been strong political resistance to treating crimes by men against women as hate crimes."

Sexual Orientation

Discrimination and prejudice based on sexual orientation is the most recent addition to the civil rights movement, but it has not yet been fully accepted as an equal. Since the 1970s, gay men and lesbians have demanded the same protection against discrimination as blacks, Jews, women, and other groups; they have demanded recognition as a victimized minority. Although some states and municipalities have enacted laws prohibiting discrimination against homosexuals, many states and the federal government do not have any laws extending civil rights protection to homosexuals. The Supreme Court has held that states can make it a crime for adult homosexuals to engage in voluntary sexual relations. The president of the United States has ordered that military personnel who are open about their homosexuality be dismissed from the armed forces for that reason alone.

So how should criminal law react to the ambivalence of American political institutions? How should the criminal law regard crime by prejudiced heterosexuals against homosexuals? If that is a hate crime, then is it also a hate crime whenever one person attacks another because he or she dislikes (hates) that person's sexual practices?

Considering all the different contexts where discrimination against gays and lesbians occurs, none is more compelling than the criminal context, with its bloody legacy of "gay bashing." Whatever arguments might be made to deny gays and lesbians protection against discrimination in housing and employment, it is hard to imagine any coherent argument in favor of their exclusion from the hate crime umbrella. Indeed, such exclusion would rightly be perceived by gays and lesbians as a case of blatant governmental discrimination.

There are many other prejudices toward which American society has become more sensitive in the past several decades. One prominent example is ageism—prejudice and discrimination against the elderly. Senior citizens, through their lobbying organization, the American Association of Retired Persons, have become a powerful political force, and they have achieved considerable success in having age discrimination prohibited. If crime based upon race discrimination is an especially heinous crime, then many people will no doubt conclude that crime based upon ageism ought also to be a hate crime trigger. The same kind of logic no doubt will lead advocates for the physically and mentally handicapped, undocumented aliens, HIV positive persons, and others to demand special condemnation and extra punishment for criminals who victimize them. Thus, the creation of hate crime laws and jurisprudence will inevitably generate a contentious politics about which prejudices count and which do not. Creating a hate crime jurisprudence forces us to proclaim which prejudices are worse than others, itself an exercise in prejudice. This controversy will really have little to do with appropriate sentencing for criminals and everything to do with the comparative symbolic status of various groups.

The Causal Link

For criminal conduct to constitute a hate crime, it must be motivated by prejudice and there must be a *causal relationship* between the criminal conduct and the officially designated prejudice. Must the criminal conduct have been totally, primarily, substantially, or just slightly caused by prejudiced motivation? If the criminal conduct must be motivated by prejudice to the exclusion of all other motivating factors, there will not be much hate crime. Contrariwise, if the hate crime designation is satisfied by a showing of merely a slight relationship between prejudice and criminal conduct, a great deal of crime by members of one group against members of another group will be labeled as hate crime.

Vandalism or criminal mischief involving the defacement of public and private property presents another complicated problem. A great deal of graffiti, in public and private, expresses disparaging opinions of women, gays and lesbians, Jews, blacks, and other minorities, whites, and other social categories. Should the act of scrawling such graffiti be included in the hate crime accounting system and trigger special condemnation and extra punishment? For example, should anti-homosexual graffiti scrawled on a bathroom wall be counted as a hate crime, or should it only count as hate crime if the graffiti is directed at an individual, institution, or place identified with a particular group (e.g., anti-homosexual graffiti on a gay man's home, anti-homosexual vandalism on an AIDS center, or anti-Semitic graffiti in a Jewish cemetery)?

Should hate crimes include the use of racist, sexist, homophobic, and other disparaging epithets combined with in-your-face shouting, gesticulating, and threatening conduct that occurs all too often in the context of ad hoc arguments and fights on playgrounds, streets, and in the workplace? Consider the following incident involving two neighbors, a white woman and a

> *"For criminal conduct to constitute a hate crime, it must be motivated by prejudice."*

Hispanic woman, which was reported to the New York City Bias Incident Investigation Unit. According to the Hispanic woman, her white neighbor insulted and harassed her with anti-Hispanic epithets. After investigating, the police declined to label the incident a "bias crime" because the neighbors had been engaged in an on-going dispute over building code violations and the epithets had been uttered during a heated argument on this same subject. In Queens, New York, the following incident was treated as a bias crime. A gay male couple knocked on their neighbor's door and asked him to turn down the music, which was so loud it shook the walls. The neighbor refused and hurled anti-gay epithets. Is this a hate crime?

Some instances like this do not qualify as crimes at all because they do not pass the threshold that separates offensive speech from criminal conduct. But other instances could be classified as criminal harassment or intimidation. Does hate crime include or exclude mixed speech/conduct? . . .

Defining Hate Crimes

"Hate crime" is a social construct. It is a new term, which is neither familiar nor self-defining. Coined in the late 1980s to emphasize criminal conduct motivated by prejudice, it focuses on the psyche of the criminal rather than on the criminal's conduct. It attempts to extend the civil rights paradigm into the world of crime and criminal law.

How much hate crime there is and what the appropriate response should be depends upon how hate crime is conceptualized and defined. In constructing a definition of hate crime, choices must be made regarding the meaning of prejudice and the nature of the causal link between the offender's prejudice and criminal conduct.

> *"How much hate crime there is and what the appropriate response should be depends upon how hate crime is conceptualized and defined."*

"Prejudice" is an amorphous term. If prejudice is defined narrowly, to include only certain organized hate-based ideologies, there will be very little hate crime. If prejudice is defined broadly, a high percentage of intergroup crimes will qualify as hate crimes. If only a select few crimes, such as assault or harassment, can be transformed into hate crimes, the number of hate crimes will be small. If vandalism and graffiti, when motivated by prejudice, count as hate crimes, the number of hate crimes will be enormous. If criminal conduct must be completely or predominantly caused by prejudice in order to be termed hate crime, there will be few hate crimes. If prejudice need only *in part* to have motivated the crime, hate crime will be plentiful. In other words, we can make the hate crime problem as small or large as we desire by manipulating the definition.

There are many different types of prejudices that might qualify for hate crime designation. Some civil rights and affirmative action legislation speak in terms of "protected groups," but this does not easily apply in the hate crime context because when it comes to crime, all victims are a protected group. Why should some victims be considered more protected than others?

Hate Crimes Are a Serious Problem

by William J. Clinton

About the author: *William J. Clinton is the forty-second president of the United States.*

Those of us who grew up in the segregated south are perhaps more sensitive to all these various hate crimes issues because we grew up in a culture that was dominated for too long by people who thought they only counted if they had somebody to look down on; that they could only lift themselves up if they were pushing someone else down; that their whole definition of a positive life required a negative definition of another group of people. That's really what this is all about. . . .

Oppression

When you strip it all away, down deep inside there is this idea that you cannot organize personal life or social life unless some group feels better about itself only when they are oppressing someone else.

Or people at least believe that they ought to have the right to do violence against someone else solely because of who they are, not because of what they do.

Now at the bottom, that's what this is all about. And I have said that repeatedly since I have been president. But one of the things I have sought to do in our country is to bridge all these divides and to get all of our people, not to agree with one another, not to even like one another all the time—goodness knows, we can't like everybody all the time—but to recognize that our common humanity is more important than these categorical differences. And also to recognize that over the long run, America will not be able to be a force for good abroad unless we are good at home. . . .

First of all we must always be working on ourselves.

That's really what this is about. . . . We know that inside each of us there are vulnerabilities to dehumanizing other people simply by putting them in a category that permits us to dismiss them, or that permits us to put them in a cate-

Excerpted from a speech on hate crimes given by President William J. Clinton, April 16, 1999.

gory so that on a bad day when we are feeling especially bad about something we've done, we can say, "Well, thank God, I'm not them." And it is a short step from that, a short, short step from that, to licensing or even participating in acts of violence. . . .

As I said, . . . it is very easy to get into a social system where you always get to think a little better of yourself because you've always got someone that you can dehumanize.

And that's really what this whole issue is with—with gays today in America. We're not talking about everybody agreeing with everybody else on every political issue, we're talking about whether people have a right, if they show up and work hard and obey the law and are good citizens, to pursue their lives and dignity free of fear—without fear of being abused.

And this should not be a partisan issue. . . . This ought not to be anything other than a basic, central statement of American principle.

The Number One Security Threat

But I would like to say one other thing, just as a practical matter. Isn't it interesting to you that we are on the eve of a new century in a new millennium which will be largely characterized by globalization, the explosion of technology, especially in information, in the integration of people, and the number one security threat to that is the persistence of old, even primitive hatreds?

Don't you think that's interesting?

So what I worry about all the time is whether terrorists can get on the Internet and figure out how to make

> *"The number one security threat . . . is the persistence of old, even primitive hatreds."*

chemical and biological weapons to pursue agendas against people of different ethnic or religious groups.

And so it's very humbling, I think, for those of us who think we have brought the modern world and prosperity and rationality to all of human affairs, to see what is going on in the Balkans, and to see these terrible examples of violence here in our own country. It's very humbling. We should remember that each of us almost wakes up every day with the scales of light and darkness in our own hearts, and we've got to keep them in proper balance.

And we have to be in the United States absolutely resolute about this. That's why I think this hate crimes issue is so important.

That's why I convened the first White House Conference on Hate Crimes a year and a half ago [November 1997].

A Progress Report

Since then, I would like to say we have substantially increased the number of FBI agents working on these crimes. We have successfully prosecuted a number of serious cases. We have formed local hate crime working groups in U.S. attorneys' offices around the country. But this is a significant problem.

In 1997, the last year for which we have statistics, over 8,000 hate crime incidents were reported in the United States. That's almost one an hour. Almost one an hour. So, what are we going to do about it? I'd like to mention . . . three other things.

New Initiatives

I've asked the Justice Department and the Education Department to include in their annual report on school safety crucial information on hate crimes among young people both at and away from school, not only to warn but to educate.

Secondly, I'm asking the Department of Education to collect important data for the first time on hate crimes and bias on college campuses. Another cruel irony, isn't it? College, the place where we're supposed to have the most freedom, the place where we're supposed to be the most

> *"The larger mission is to change the mind, the heart, and the habits of our people when they're young to keep bad things from happening."*

rational, the place where we're supposed to be able to think the highest thoughts with the greatest amount of space. We have significant hate crime problems there. And we need to shine the light on that.

Third—I'm very pleased about this—we are going to have a public/private partnership to help reach middle school students to discuss this whole issue with them and talk about tolerance, why it is a moral as well as a practical imperative.

And the partnership includes AT&T, Court TV, the National Middle School Association, the Anti-Defamation League, Cable in the Classrooms, as well as the Departments of Education and Justice.

I would like to thank them all, because we have to not only punish bad things when they happen, but the larger mission is to change the mind, the heart and the habits of our people when they're young to keep bad things from happening.

Finally, let me join the others . . . in saying Congress should pass this law [Hate Crimes Prevention Act]. . . . The federal laws already punish some crimes committed against people on the basis of race or religion or national origin, but . . . not all crimes are committed for that purpose. This would strengthen and expand the ability of the Justice Department by removing needless jurisdictional requirements for resisting crimes and giving federal prosecutors the ability to prosecute hate crimes committed because of sexual orientation, gender or disability, along with race and religion.

Doing What Is Right

Now again I say, when we get exercised about these things, in particular when someone dies in a horrible incident in America, or when we see slaughter or ethnic cleansing abroad, we should remember that we defeat these things by teaching and by practicing a different way of life, and by reacting vigorously when they occur within our own midst. That is what this is about.

And we should remember whenever we ourselves commit even a small slip where we dehumanize or demonize someone else who is different from us that every society must teach, practice and react if you want to make the most of the world toward which we are moving.

Our diversity is a godsend for us in the world of the 21st century, but it is also the potential for the old, haunting demons that are hard to root out of the human spirit.

The Hate Crimes Prevention Act will be important substantively and symbolically to send a message to ourselves and to the world that we are going into 21st century determined to preach and to practice what is right.

Hate Crimes Against Gays Are a Serious Problem

by Dan Quinn

About the author: *Dan Quinn is a writer for the* Advocate, *a national gay and lesbian newsmagazine.*

As gay men and lesbians prepare to take part in annual gay pride events, antiviolence activists are bracing for another annual occurrence: a spike in antigay hate crimes. The phenomenon is, sadly, easy to predict, the activists say.

"Often it's very pronounced and very direct," says Tracey Conaty, field organizer for the Washington D.C.–based National Gay and Lesbian Task Force. "As soon as visibility increases, so does the violence."

Gay Pride

Part of the reason for high rates of antigay hate crimes in June, when many cities traditionally celebrate gay pride, is that the summer months draw more people outside, increasing the potential pool of crime targets and perpetrators. Nonetheless, the apparent link between higher gay visibility and increased antigay violence can be startling: In the Boston area in June 1996, for example, three gay men were killed the weekend after the city's gay pride parade sparked a bitter debate about homosexuality in the mainstream press. Gay activists were left to speculate about the effects of the public acrimony, wondering just how much it had contributed to the killings.

And pride parades aren't the only examples of a correlation between visibility and violence. Bea Hanson, director of client services at the New York City Gay and Lesbian Anti-violence Project, recalls when antigay violence in New York City rose during an especially divisive debate in 1992 over how homosexuality should be addressed in the city's public schools. "That was the first year that our incidence [of reported antigay hate crimes] didn't go down after the summer," Hanson says.

Violence can also rise during election campaigns on antigay referenda. In 1992, for example, the reported incidence of antigay violence increased in Ore-

Reprinted from "The Crime That's Not Necessarily a Crime," by Dan Quinn, *The Advocate,* June 10, 1997. Reprinted with permission.

gon and Colorado as debate heated up over measures that sought to deny any civil rights protections to gays and lesbians on the basis of their sexual orientation. During a subsequent attempt to pass another such referendum in Oregon, a lesbian and a gay man were killed when the home they shared was firebombed. And in 1995 in Maine, activists reported that yard signs in opposition to an antigay referendum were riddled with bullet holes.

Nationally, reported antigay hate crimes increased by 6% in 1996 over the previous year, according to a March 11 report. But officials of the National Coalition of Anti-Violence Programs, which compiled the report from information provided by 14 antiviolence programs around the country, say they aren't surprised by the increase. They point to inflammatory election-year rhetoric over same-sex marriage and the Supreme Court's ruling against Colorado's Amendment 2: Both issues kept gays and lesbians in the public eye for much of the year.

Attacking a Sense of Identity

That expressions of gay pride can lead to antigay violence may seem ironic. The irony deepens in consideration of the psychological toll exacted by such violence, which can renew doubts and fears among gays and lesbians about their sexual orientation that they may have long ago put behind them.

"Hate crimes attack a basic part of the victims' identity—their sense of who they are and of the community in which they belong," says Gregory Herek, a research psychologist at the University of California, Davis. "Most lesbians and gay men have gone through a coming-out process that includes having to overcome their own sense that being gay is a bad thing. From the perspective of a victim, a hate crime can feel like an instance of being punished directly and in a very dramatic way for being gay."

Herek's research indicates that victims of antigay hate crimes suffer deeper and longer periods of psychological distress—including depression, stress, and anger—than do gay and lesbian victims of comparable, non-bias-related crimes. Worse is that the damage from hate crimes extends far beyond targeted individuals, victimizing, in effect, the entire community, says Rob Knight, executive director of El Paso, Texas–based Lambda Services, which operates a national hotline for victims of antigay hate crimes.

> *"Victims of antigay hate crimes suffer deeper and longer periods of psychological distress . . . than do gay and lesbian victims of comparable, non-bias-related crimes."*

"The perpetrator of a hate crime didn't necessarily pick the lesbian in the parking lot because he didn't like her hairstyle," Knight says. "He picked her because she's gay. Anybody in that group could have been a victim, and everybody realizes that, so the entire group suffers."

Hate-Crime Laws

In an effort to prevent antigay violence, activists are pushing for new laws in statehouses and in Congress. But those efforts beg the question. Do laws against antigay hate crimes really work? The short answer is that no one knows. The report by the antiviolence coalition shows that reported antigay bias crimes are on the rise even in areas with laws against them.

In fact, some argue that hate-crime laws are not the answer for stopping the violence. For one thing, determining the true motivation for a crime is often difficult, hindering prosecution under such laws. In addition, says Karen Franklin, a research psychologist in Oakland, California, in the real world, criminals don't calculate their moves based on the specific punishment they will suffer if caught: "When people are committing these kinds of crimes, they're not thinking on that level."

> *"Hate crimes reflect the belief that the lives of gays and lesbians simply don't matter."*

But supporters say the laws have important benefits—even if current laws haven't been on the books long enough for those benefits to be reflected in crime statistics. For one thing, they help keep at least some of the gay-bashers off the streets—a goal that is all the more important since research shows that people who commit hate crimes often are repeat offenders. "Those who are prosecuted and convicted of these crimes spend more time in jail or have stiffer sentences handed to them, says Winnie Stachelberg, legislative director for the gay lobbying group, Human Rights Campaign. "And, obviously, I think that's a terribly important message."

Laws against hate crimes are only part of the solution, however. Pushing for more police training—on gay and lesbian issues as well as on hate crimes—is another priority. Also important is overcoming the fear many gay and lesbian victims have of reporting hate crimes to police in the first place.

But whatever the limitations of strong hate-crime laws, there's a fundamental reason to push for them, argues Dianne Hardy-Garcia, executive director for the Lesbian/Gay Rights Lobby of Texas, an Austin-based political group: Hate crimes reflect the belief that the lives of gays and lesbians simply don't matter. And in the end, she says, "how do we get employment or other protections if they don't even value our lives?"

Hate Crimes Against Women Are a Serious Problem

by Patt Morrison

About the author: *Patt Morrison is a columnist for the* Los Angeles Times.

First you see the guy in the T-shirt following the teenage girl in the store. She glances back at him and keeps going. He hustles up and shoves her, really hard, into a rack of shoes. When she looks to see what the hell happened, he's glaring and ranting and coming at her as she backs off, and then he goes past her and out the door; it's all there on the video from the security camera.

If this had happened only once, the charge would be a misdemeanor. But five times now, at the beach, in downtown San Diego, in stores, to five women, all strangers to the man in the T-shirt—as the San Diego County deputy district attorney sees it, that's a string of felony hate crimes, committed because the victims were women. And he's prosecuting the man in the T-shirt as the suspect in all of them.

What Is a Hate Crime?

We know what a hate crime is, don't we?

It's shooting up a community center because the sign out front says "Jewish." It's dragging a black man behind a truck until his head comes off. In October 1999, we're watching a jury being seated in Wyoming for the murder trial of one of the men who confessed to pummeling a gay college student into a coma before the victim was left hanging on a wooden fence to die.

And yet here is the San Diego case, filed under a rarely used 1992 state law that extends hate crime statutes to gender-provoked crimes. Even for Hector Jimenez, who prosecutes hate crimes for San Diego County, it's a first, based on "the fact that [the suspect] is committing crimes somewhat randomly against women who don't know him, with no provocation, no sexual desires or sexual motives, no financial motive. The motive seems to be to attack women."

What is the standard of proof for a gender hate crime? Is it the difference between a thug snarling, "Shut up or I'll pop you one," or "Shut up or I'll pop you one, *bitch*"? Does a gender hate crime require a pattern, or can it be a single incident, as one burning cross on a black family's lawn can be sufficient evidence of hate?

The U.S. Supreme Court is even now considering the constitutionality of the 1994 federal Violence Against Women Act, which lets some battery and rape cases be categorized as hate crimes so the victims can sue their attackers.

And in 1999, in the sweaty heat of a Beltway August, a woman named Carole Carrington testified on Capitol Hill, asking Congress to shore up federal gender hate crime laws.

Her daughter, her granddaughter and a family friend were simply tourists visiting the winter beauties of Yosemite when they disappeared—spirited off and murdered. The man who confessed to killing them, Carrington testified shakily, "claims to have fantasized about killing women for the last 30 years." They died, said their mother, grandmother, friend, "simply because they were women."

History Lessons

Put the lens of gender hate crime to your eye and history, recent and distant, takes on an altogether different cast.

The ancient Romans' mass rape of the Sabine women—a favorite subject in classical art because it permitted painting naked women for aesthetic purposes—becomes a class-action hate crime. What of Bluebeard, or Henry VIII, who discarded or killed wives for not bringing forth sons (the Tudor monarch did not know, nor would he have likely believed, that sperm determines a fetus' gender)?

Every mass murderer or serial killer with a "woman problem" could be shifted from mere "maniac" to the more sensible and comprehensible category of hate criminal: Jack the Ripper, Richard Speck, Ted Bundy.

There was more than murder afoot when a man burst into the engineering building at the University of Montreal 10 years ago, separated the students by gender, and opened fire

> *"Put the lens of gender hate crime to your eye and history, recent and distant, takes on an altogether different cast."*

on the women, screaming obscenities about "feminists." He killed 14 women. When a Texas man opened fire in a cafeteria in 1991, he went table to table choosing females to shoot. Both men left behind letters telling how much they despised women.

The laws are so new that the standards are still in flux. Is it a law only for strangers? When do domestic crimes qualify as hate crimes? Is a man beating just his ex-wife, or is he beating every woman who ever stood him up? Is he killing a woman, or Women?

And where, the question must be asked, would the Y chromosome victim rank the male victims of the rare female serial killer?

A Justice Department attorney said that the law would not mean the Feds would prosecute every rape and wife beating—only violent outrages with indisputable gender hatred at the core.

Still, some gaze on the expanding range of hate crimes and ask in dismay where it will all end. Their question should be asked not of the laws, but of the crimes that put them on the books in the first place.

All Hate Crimes Are a Serious Problem

by Susan Raffo

About the author: *Susan Raffo is a freelance writer.*

Like many others, I attended a vigil in my hometown to honor Matthew Shepard. [Shepard, a gay college student, was robbed, beaten, tied to a fence post, and left for dead in Wyoming in October 1998.] This vigil was a perfect example of the organizing power contained within the Gay Lesbian Bisexual Transgender (GLBT) community. Within three days, a site had been selected, a full outdoor sound system found, a series of speakers scheduled, and a massive phone and email notification system initiated. When it was raining heavily a few hours before the vigil, an alternative site—a large Episcopalian church nearby—was found and the entire vigil moved inside. By 7:30 P.M. the church was standing room only and there were over 100 people outside. Candles had been donated by the Target stores and the Gay Men's Chorus had organized to sing. The evening was a moving piece of community organizing.

I got there early and sat where I could watch people enter. Some entered the church with visible grief, their body movements solemn and their eyes downcast. Others walked in, looked for familiar faces and called with pleasure to friends and colleagues, their laughter as present as the murmur of hushed voices. Once the program began, the speakers moved from focusing specifically on Matthew Shepard and the cause of anti-gay violence to discussing the upcoming election and its importance to the GLBT community. Throughout the evening, I could see and hear people crying, the soft sounds of their weeping creating a back beat to the voices speaking from the pulpit.

A Powerful Event

The vigil was a powerful event and it manifest a force that is still growing, a force determined to instill legislation that recognizes hate crimes on the basis of sexual orientation.

But I have to admit that, along with my grief at the death of Matthew Shepard

Reprinted from "Thinking About Hate Crimes," by Susan Raffo, Z *Magazine*, January 1999. Reprinted with permission.

and my heightened awareness of the forces of hate gathered against the bodies of GLBT people, I also felt a sadness not connected to these things. One of the early speakers that evening, a woman who works as an anti-violence coordinator for a local agency, stated that violence on the basis of sexual orientation or gender expression is the third largest form of hate crime in the United States, totaling 11 percent of all recorded hate crimes. This comment fed my growing discomfort.

Other Victims

I took part in an evening of reflection, an evening in which the existence of hate crimes was loudly and repeatedly denounced, and only briefly was mention made of those who experience an even greater likelihood of being the victims of hate crimes than GLBT people: immigrants and people of color. We know that after Matthew Shepard was brutally beaten, the same college students attacked two Latinos and pistol-whipped them with the same gun they used on Matthew.

For the perpetrators, the connection between Matthew Shepard and the bodies of the two Latino men was direct and understood. But for my community, the community who gathered to denounce the death of a young man we perceive to be one of our own, that connection seemed to be mostly lost.

My sadness is about what happens when, in the wildness of grief, we are called to imagine our own and to feel protective of them.

No Hate Crime Should Be Tolerated

It is not right that, during the vigil, an entire evening could be spent discussing the victims of hate crimes and only mention hate crimes on the basis of sexual orientation. It's not right that when, as a group we shouted, "we will not tolerate these crimes," we were only verbally referring to crimes on the basis of sexual orientation and, for some, gender expression. We should not be able to easily distinguish between different types of hate crimes. We should not be able to separate one form from another, saying homophobia without saying racism or anti-immigrant, saying Matthew Shepard without saying James Byrd. Indeed, often the hate crimes themselves are not distinguishable. It would be impossible to say, when a gay person of color is attacked or a lesbian—both white and of color—is attacked, that the motivation for that crime is only the victim's sexual orientation. Race and sex must be equally involved and, for all we know, might be the motivating factor that caused the perpetrator to strike out.

> *"It is not more painful or more horrible to be beaten or murdered due to our sexual orientation than it is to be the victim of violence on the basis of our race or nationality."*

There is no doubt in my mind that we must have laws that recognize hate crimes on the basis of sexual orientation and gender expression. These laws are desperately needed and the flare-up of violence directed at GLBT people in the wake of Matthew Shepard's death is further evidence of this. But this is only one part of the political and emotional moment in which we are sitting. A primary strategy of the right wing has been to put a wedge between GLBT civil rights movements and the civil rights movements of other groups, most specifically, African-American civil rights groups and churches.

> *"Hatred must be confronted no matter what form it takes or what person is under attack."*

We cannot afford to contribute to this imagined chasm. It is not more painful or more horrible to be beaten or murdered due to our sexual orientation than it is to be the victim of violence on the basis of our race or nationality or for any other reason. Each of these crimes is designed to silence more than the individual being attacked: hate crimes intend to frighten into silence a whole community. As Matthew Shepard's attackers demonstrated by their actions: hate is hate and the fact that Matthew died while the Latino men did not could well be about nothing more than the fact that Matthew was alone and Matthew was attacked first.

Hatred Must Be Confronted

We have the opportunity to show the forces of hate in this country that we respond at moments like this one with the awareness of our connection to others who experience hate. There are many of us who are at risk of being victimized because of who we are and not all of that "us" are gay, lesbian, bisexual or transgendered. When we close our eyes and imagine the bodies of those who, in our grief, we feel moved to protect, let many people dwell in our hearts. When in our communities, we hear of those who are beaten or murdered because of their color or because they were not born in this country, let us remember Matthew and feel moved to speak out, using the power of our organizing force to work against all hate crimes, knowing that hatred must be confronted no matter what form it takes or what person is under attack.

Hate Crimes Are Not a Serious Problem

by Samuel Francis

About the author: *Samuel Francis is a nationally syndicated columnist.*

Hatred, hatred everywhere, and so little time for the federal leviathan to do anything about it! Nevertheless, just about every prominent political person [has] denounced "hate" in one way or another. President Bill Clinton denounced it, telling a mass gathering of homosexual supporters that hate is "America's largest problem."

Democratic presidential candidate Bill Bradley also denounced hate, telling yet another mass gathering of homosexual supporters that "we have to oppose any manifestations of hatred with undiminished fervor whenever and wherever it occurs," and both he and the president demanded enactment of new federal "hate crime" laws. Republican Sen. Orrin Hatch, not to be outdone in hatred of hate, also denounces hate, sponsoring legislation to curb Internet sites that advocate hate and violence. All in all, you could say hate really took it on the chin.

Well, some hate did, that is. As the *Washington Post* pointed out, Bradley cited the "same hate crimes the president listed," which included the murder of homosexual Matthew Shepard in Wyoming and of James Byrd, a black man, in Texas in 1998, as well as shootings at a Jewish community center in Los Angeles in 1999.

Neither politician, of course, bothered to mention the shootings at a Christian church in Fort Worth in September 1999, a massacre that left seven people dead. Murdering Christians is not "hate," you see, especially if they are also white. Had the attack in Fort Worth been on members of a black church, we could have expected not only a presidential speech about it but also a most lucrative fund-raising campaign by Morris Dees [the founder of the hate-watch group, Southern Poverty Law Center] and other professional witch hunters of the left.

Reprinted from "Hatred of 'Hate' Often Masks an Agenda," by Samuel Francis, *Conservative Chronicle*, October 20, 1999. Reprinted with permission of Samuel Francis and Creators Syndicate.

Of course, there is nothing wrong with denouncing "hate," if real "hate" is what you're denouncing. But the politically convenient selection of some victims of "hate" and the exclusion or omission of others suggests that real "hate" is not what is being denounced.

Clinton's claim that hate is "America's largest problem" also suggests that there's something else being talked about besides real hate. Despite occasional murders driven purely by hatred of one sort of group or another, it is preposterous to claim that hate is "America's largest problem." The number of "hate crimes" enumerated by the FBI for 1997, the most recent year for which data are available, was some 9,800. A substantial number of these (4,100 or 42 percent) were not violent in any way, and even the total number is less than 1 percent of the 13 million serious crimes reported that year.

A Political Agenda

What is being talked about when "hate" is brought up, of course, is a political agenda. If you can stick the hate label on anyone who criticizes homosexuality as an immoral or abnormal practice, anyone who opposes immigration, and anyone who objects to affirmative action or civil rights policy, then you've effectively silenced them and engineered a monopoly of the dialogue for your own point of view.

It's one thing to denounce the real criminals and crimes Clinton and Bradley denounced, but there's little point in denouncing them at all.

> *"[Hate] becomes a 'problem' only if what you mean is not real 'hate'. . . but various political, moral, religious or social attitudes and ideas that you oppose."*

Those criminals, and others like them, are punished quickly and severely, and indifference to, or leniency toward them and their acts, is simply not a problem.

"Hate" becomes a "problem," a subject appropriate for political discussion, only if it means something other than the brutal criminal deeds Clinton and Bradley mentioned. It becomes a "problem" only if what you mean is not real "hate"—an obsessive and irrational dislike of certain groups that breeds violence against them—but various political, moral, religious or social attitudes and ideas that you oppose and wish to suppress.

That is why Bradley's rant that "We have to oppose any manifestations of hatred with undiminished fervor whenever and wherever it occurs" and Hatch's ill-advised bill against "hate" on the Internet are really rather frightening. If they were really concerned about real "hate," there wouldn't be any problem with what they're saying, but then, if that's what they were really concerned with, there wouldn't be any need for what they say or want to do. The consequences in action of real "hate" are merely matters for the police and the courts, not for political oratory and new legislation.

If it's real hate you want, watch Harvard's Alan Dershowitz screaming that

Pat Buchanan isn't a "human being" on public television. Dershowitz is not the kind of "manifestation of hatred" that Bradley and Clinton were talking about, any more than the Fort Worth killings of Christians were, and he can't be prosecuted for "hate"—not yet, anyway. But if Clinton, Bradley and Hatch get the laws against the phony kind of "hate" they're demanding, even Dershowitz might find himself in need of a good lawyer.

Hate Crime Statistics Are Misleading

by Jared Taylor

About the author: *Jared Taylor is a journalist and author of* Paved with Good Intentions: The Failure of Race Relations in Contemporary America.

The idea of "hate" crimes and the increased penalties attached to them are a radical departure from traditional criminal justice in that they punish certain motivations more than others. Increased penalties are justified by pointing out that the law has always taken a criminal's state of mind into account: Was the killing deliberate or an accident? Was it planned in cold blood or done in the heat of the moment? However, these are questions of *intent*, and intent is, indeed, a factor in determining guilt. "Hate" crimes break new ground by considering *motive*. Traditionally the law does not care about motive. You are just as guilty of murder whether you kill a man because he stole your wife, blackmailed you, or stepped on your toe.

Hate crime laws require that the courts search for certain motives and add extra penalties if they find them. Therefore, if you punch a man in the nose because he took your parking spot or because he was unbearably ugly or because you just felt like punching someone that day, you are guilty of assault. If you say "nigger" and punch a black man you are guilty of a hate crime and are punished more severely. Like almost all recent innovations in morals, what started with race has expanded to "sexual orientation" and even disabilities like blindness or feeble-mindedness.

The Hate Crime Statistics Act

Ever since 1990, when Congress passed the Hate Crime Statistics Act, the FBI has been charged with collecting national statistics on criminal acts "motivated, in whole or in part, by bias." The law does not force local police departments to supply this information but most do. In 1997, the most recent year for which data are available, the FBI received "hate crime" information from 11,211 local agencies serving more than 83 percent of the United States population.

Reprinted with permission from "The Great Hate Crimes Hoax," by Jared Taylor, *American Renaissance,* July 1999. Additional information available by writing P.O. Box 527, Oakton, VA 22124, or visiting www.amren.com.

That year, there was a total of 9,861 "hate crimes," of which 6,981 were based on race or ethnic origin The rest were for reasons of religion (1,493, of which 1,159 were anti-Jewish), sexual orientation (1,375, of which 14 were anti-heterosexual), or disability (12).

The FBI reports 8,474 suspected offenders whose race was known—5,344 were white and 1,629 were black. Their crimes can be divided into violent and nonviolent offenses, and by calculating rates we find that blacks were 1.99 times more likely than whites to commit hate crimes in general and 2.24 times more likely to commit violent hate crimes. This overrepresentation of blacks in hate crimes, not just in race bias cases but in all categories, runs counter to the common impression that whites are the virtually exclusive perpetrators of hate crimes and are certainly more likely to commit them than blacks.

The real significance of "hate" crimes, however, is their small number. Of the 6,981 offenses based on race or ethnicity, only 4,105 were violent, involving murder, rape, robbery, or assault. The rest were such things as vandalism and intimidation. These numbers are almost insignificant compared to the 1,766,000 interracial crimes of violence (combining both single- and multiple-offender offenses) reported in the Department of Justice survey for 1994.

How important is the distinction between interracial crimes that are officially designated as hate crimes and those that are not? For a crime to be considered a hate crime, the perpetrator must make his motive clear, usually by saying something nasty. It is not hard to imagine that of the nearly two million interracial crimes committed in 1994, some—perhaps even a great many—were "motivated, in whole or in part, by bias" but the perpetrators didn't bother to say so.

Given the realities of race in the United States, would it be unreasonable for someone attacked by a criminal of a different race to wonder whether race had something to do with the attack, even if his assailant said nothing? Such suspicions are even more likely in the case of the 490,266 acts of *group* violence that crossed racial lines in 1994. A white woman gang-raped by blacks or a black man cornered and beaten by whites will think he was singled out at least in part because of race, even if the attackers said nothing.

Hate crime laws assume that special harm is done to society when people are attacked because of race. But which does more damage to society: the few thousand violent acts officially labeled as hate crimes or the *millions* of ordinary interracial

> *"Which does more harm to society: the few thousand violent acts officially labeled as hate crimes or the **millions of ordinary interracial crimes of violence?**"*

crimes of violence—90 percent of which are committed by blacks against whites? If race relations are so fragile they must be protected with laws that add extra penalties to race-related crimes, why not automatically add extra penalties to *any* interracial crime, on the assumption that it harmed race relations? The problem, of course, is that most of the people slapped with heavier penalties would be black.

Hispanics

Official thinking about "hate crimes" suffers from another crushing defect. As Joseph Fallon, who has written for *AR* [*American Renaissance*] has noted, the FBI reports hate crimes *against* Hispanics but not *by* Hispanics. In the forms the FBI has local police departments fill out, Hispanics are clearly indicated as a victim category but they are not an option as a perpetrator category when the FBI asks for "Suspected Race of Offender." The FBI therefore forces local police departments to categorize most Hispanics as "white." Official figures for 1997 reflect this. The total number of "hate crimes" for that year—9,861—includes 636 crimes of anti-Hispanic bias, but not one of the 8,474 known offenders is "Hispanic" because the FBI's data collection method doesn't permit such a designation.

If someone goes after a Mexican because he doesn't like Mexicans it is an anti-Hispanic crime. If the same Mexican commits a "hate crime" against a white, both the victim *and* the perpetrator are considered white. And, in fact, the 1997 FBI figures duly record 214 "white" offenders who committed anti-white hate crimes! The offenders were undoubtedly Hispanic, but the report doesn't say so. Some of the "whites" who are reported to have committed hate crimes against blacks and homosexuals are almost certainly Hispanic, but there is no way to be sure.

> *"The FBI reports hate crimes against Hispanics but not by Hispanics."*

Hispanic perpetrators show up only if you investigate specific "hate" crimes. The FBI lists five cases of racially-motivated murder for 1997—three "anti-black" and two "anti-white." The report says nothing about the perpetrators or the circumstances of the killings, so *AR* got the details from the local police departments.

Two of the anti-black killings took place in the same town, a mostly Hispanic suburb of Los Angeles called Hawaiian Gardens. Hawaiian Gardens has a history of black-Hispanic tension that is so bad many blacks have cleared out. In one of the 1997 murders, a 24-year-old black man was beaten to death by a mob of 10 to 14 Hispanics who took turns smashing his head with a baseball bat. In the other, a Hispanic gang member challenged a 29-year-old black man's right to be in the neighborhood. A few minutes later he came back and shot the man in the chest. In both cases, the victims and killers did not know each other and the motivation appears to have been purely racial. These crimes are typical of what we think of as hate crime murders, but because no Hispanics are identified as perpetrators in the FBI report, the killers were classified as white.

The third anti-black killing took place in Anchorage, Alaska. A white man, Brett Maness, killed his neighbor, a black man, Delbert White, after a brief struggle. Mr. Maness, who was growing marijuana in his apartment and kept an arsenal of weapons, had been shooting a pellet gun at Mr. White's house, and the black came over to complain. Interestingly, a jury found that Mr. Maness killed Mr. White in self-defense. The incident—which sounds rather ambiguous—was classified as a hate crime because Mr. Maness had shouted racial slurs at Mr. White in the past and because "racist" literature was found in his apartment.

The remaining two killings were classified as anti-white, but only one fits the usual idea of these crimes. Four white men were walking on a street in Palm Beach, Florida, when a car came to a stop not far from them. Two black men got out with their hands behind their backs and one said "What are you crackers looking at?" One of the white men replied, "Not you, nigger," whereupon one of the blacks brought a gun from behind his back and fired several times, killing one white and wounding another. Attackers and victims did not know each other, and the motivation appears to have been purely racial. The other anti-white killing involved a Texas businessman from India, Sri Punjabi, who shot his Mexican daugh-

> *"[The FBI] inflates the number of hate crimes committed by 'whites' by calling Hispanics white, and suggests that Hispanics never commit 'hate crimes.'"*

ter-in-law because his son had divorced an Indian wife to marry her. Mr. Punjabi was furious because his son married someone who was not Indian. (Presumably, this crime could have been classified as anti-Hispanic rather than anti-white.)

Not the Media Image

These five "hate crime" murders reported for 1997 do not exactly fit the media image of whites brutalizing nonwhites. In fact, only one perpetrator, the Alaskan, was "white" in the usually accepted sense. What was the nature of the thousands of other officially-reported hate crimes? Without examining all 9,861 of them it is impossible to say.

It is clear, though, that the FBI report gives a false impression of what is going on. It inflates the number of hate crimes committed by "whites" by calling Hispanics white, and suggests that Hispanics never commit "hate crimes." Every year, the press duly reports this nonsense. No one, apparently, ever bothers to ask why hundreds of whites are reported to be committing hate crimes against other whites. By leaving out Hispanics and blaming their crimes on whites, the FBI report paints so distorted a picture of race relations in America that it is worse than useless.

Many Hate Crimes Are Hoaxes

by Jon Sanders

About the author: *Jon Sanders is a research fellow for the Pope Center for Higher Education Reform in Research Triangle Park, North Carolina. He is also the editor of* Clarion, *a monthly journal on higher education published by the Pope Center.*

At Duke University in November 1997, a group of students hanged from a tree a black doll bearing a sign that read "Duke hasn't changed." They also covered with black paint the nearby Class of 1948 granite bench. The site of the mock lynching was the gathering place for members of the Black Student Alliance, who had been planning a protest outside the office of Duke President Nan Keohane.

The identities of the perpetrators—evidently white racists—were unknown for nearly a week, and the campus reaction to the incident was one of horror and dismay. The *Chronicle,* Duke's student newspaper, published a letter from undergraduate Stephen Poon denouncing the episode as a "racial crime." Members of the BSA claimed that it showed how tense race relations were on campus.

Several days later the truth was out: the perpetrators were not racist whites, but blacks looking to create an impression of racism on campus. Instead of being condemned, the guilty parties were unconditionally defended by their ideological kin: "The idea behind the act," wrote Worokya Diomande in the *Chronicle,* "is being overlooked (as is usually the case). The University has not changed. Blacks are allowed to be enrolled here, but the idea is the equivalent of the transition from field slave to house slave."

A New Trend

There is a new trend on college campuses: not of hate crimes, but of students and faculty creating make-believe racist and anti-gay incidents to illustrate, as the phrase goes, "that hate could happen here," and of students, faculty, and administrators using the fictional crimes as "evidence" of the urgency of their multicultural agenda.

At Eastern New Mexico University, threatening posters started appearing around campus last September 1997. "Are you sick of queers polluting this great land with there [sic] filth?" asked the error-ridden fliers. "I thought so. Want to do something? Join the Fist of God. With his might, we can ride [sic] the world of there [sic] sickness. Ask around. We'll find you." The poster identified eight people on campus as homosexual and concluded: "Take us seriously, or we'll begin executing one queer a week following this list."

The four men and four women listed soon received threatening e-mail messages and letters. Shortly after the posters appeared, the person whose name topped the list, a lesbian teaching assistant named Miranda Prather, was attacked in her home. She told police a masked assailant had slashed her cheek with a kitchen knife.

In the ensuing investigation, police examined surveillance footage of a nearby laundromat where the threatening fliers had been posted. Their search was ultimately successful, and they were able to identify the culprit as . . . Miranda Prather. Later, they found a knife in Miss Prather's apartment that matched the wounds in her cheek.

As in the Duke case, however, no one seemed to care that the "hate crime" was a hoax. Elizabeth Jarnagin, an editorial writer for the Amarillo *Globe-News,* continued to decry anti-gay bigotry. "Let me tell you about polluting with filth," Miss Jarnagin intoned to the poster-writer, after Prather had been exposed. "Hatred is polluting with filth. Instilling terror is polluting with filth. Bigotry is polluting with filth. . . . Few of us are as blatant about it as the Fist of God. Yet hatred and intolerance are there."

> *"There is a new trend on college campuses: not of hate crimes, but of students and faculty creating make-believe racist and anti-gay incidents."*

At the University of Georgia in 1998, resident advisor Jerry Kennedy found the door of his dormitory room on fire. Everyone concluded that a bigot had been responsible: Kennedy was openly homosexual, and his door was covered with gay-activist literature. The Lesbian, Gay, and Bisexual Student Union sent a letter to University President Michael Adams asking him to address the incident by creating a hate-crime task force and obtaining a faculty advisor for the LGBSU. Meanwhile, LGBSU members wrote messages in chalk around the Tate Student Center, including "Stop burning down our doors" and "Are you next?"

The attacks on Kennedy, meanwhile, did not stop. After the third time his door was set afire, Kennedy said he thought it was "strange that somebody, in order to get to me, would risk the lives of at least five hundred people [in the dormitory]." Asked what he thought of the LBGSU's response, Kennedy said, "It makes me feel like I'm doing the right thing, and I appreciate the support."

Shortly thereafter, the official student newspaper the *Red and Black* learned that Kennedy had been the target of 9 of the 15 hate crimes reported on campus since 1995—not just the fires, but threatening phone calls and incidents of criminal trespassing. The head of the campus police said: "He's certainly had more [harassment] than anyone else I've known of." Kennedy was arrested and charged with two counts of arson and four false reports of a crime, and a student who had been suspected of setting one of the fires was exonerated. A faculty member, dealing in race discrimination told the *Red and Black* that she "hoped the Kennedy case would not hinder dialogue about homosexuality."

Proof of Strained Race Relations?

At Guilford College, a Quaker school in Greensboro, North Carolina, the president of the Student Senate, Molly Martin, was assaulted in her office late one night in February 1998. Her assailant knocked her unconscious, opened her blouse, and wrote "nigger lover" on her chest. Miss Martin refused medical attention and asked campus security not to call the police.

The attack occurred a week after anonymous letters and fliers criticizing Miss Martin had begun to appear. Miss Martin had appointed two black students to the Senate, and fliers warned students not to vote for her unless she promised an all-black Senate. She had also led the Senate the previous semester in endorsing a proposal for the creation of a full-time director of African-American affairs at the college, whose student body of thirteen thousand includes about ninety blacks.

The incident was proof to some that the college had strained race relations. "Guilford students weren't ready to start dealing with the issues we were presenting," Edward LaMont Williams, president of the college's African-American Cultural Society, told the *Chronicle of Higher Education Daily News,* "but the incident made the campus realize that racism is a real issue on campus that needs to be dealt with."

Along with increasing security, the college pledged to hasten its selection of a director of African-American affairs, inaugurate a series of dialogues on race relations, and make changes to the curriculum to include issues of race.

Meanwhile, speculation arose that Miss Martin had staged the attack herself. The police could not recreate the incident satisfactorily. Miss Martin had never shown anyone the alleged writing on her chest or damage

> *"On American campuses . . . any hate crime will do—even if it never happened."*

to her office; she said she had cleaned things up before going to campus security. Although she had supposedly been knocked unconscious, she did not exhibit any bruising; and police said it would be very unusual for an assailant in such a case to unbutton the victim's blouse instead of ripping it or pulling it down to write on her chest.

In June 1998, Miss Martin withdrew from the school. She sent an open letter to the campus apologizing "for acts that were inappropriate and that were injurious." She was referring to her inability to perform her duties properly as Student Senate president; she did not admit to any wrongdoing concerning the alleged attack.

Meanwhile, Guilford College plans to continue to address race relations by revising the curriculum, hiring more minority faculty, and even founding an institute on race relations. On American campuses, where it is assumed that our country is soaked through with bias, any hate crime will do—even if it never happened.

Most Crimes Against Women Are Not Hate Crimes

by Cathy Young

About the author: *Cathy Young is vice president of the Women's Freedom Network and author of* Ceasefire: Why Women and Men Must Join Forces to Achieve True Equality.

The fatal beating of 21-year-old University of Wyoming student Matthew Shepard, apparently motivated at least in part by his homosexuality, has renewed the debate over hate crime legislation. The murder prompted calls from gay activists, editorial pages, and public officials, including Attorney General Janet Reno and President Bill Clinton, for passage of the Federal Hate Crimes Protection Act. This bill would allow federal prosecution of crimes motivated by hatred based on gender, sexual orientation, and disability. [The bill did not pass.]

In their book *Hate Crimes: Criminal Law and Identity Politics,* criminologists James Jacobs and Kimberly Potter argue that ordinary criminal law provides adequate protection for victims of hate crimes—a point underscored by the Shepard case, in which prosecutors plan to seek the death penalty for the accused killers. Jacobs and Potter also warn that focusing on the identity aspects of crimes with often ambiguous motives can exacerbate tensions between groups, and they note that hate crime laws raise First Amendment concerns because they tend to punish perpetrators for their beliefs. But apart from the general problems posed by laws that single out "hate" or "bias" crimes, the bill before Congress contains an especially insidious provision: the addition of gender to the existing categories of race, religion, and ethnicity.

Gender-Based Hate Crimes Are Uncommon

Except for one or two sensational cases, such as the 1989 massacre of 14 female engineering students at the University of Montreal by Marc Lepine, one would be hard pressed to think of a gender-based hate crime comparable to the murder of Shepard or of James Byrd, the black man dragged to his death behind a pickup truck in Texas in the summer of 1998. Even anti-gay violence is directed at men more than 80 percent of the time.

But many feminists argue that we simply fail to recognize the gender bias in crimes against women such as rape ("both a symbol and an act of women's subordinate social status to men," according to University of Michigan law professor Catharine MacKinnon) and domestic abuse. These theories—distilled to sheer lunacy in the work of Andrea Dworkin, who believes that women live under "a police state where every man is deputized" and that heterosexual sex is a violation by definition—may be intellectually stimulating to some, but they are far too speculative to serve as a basis for legislation.

Forensic psychology does not support the view that rapists are driven primarily by hatred toward women rather than, say, sexual compulsion or anger at the whole world. The feminist interpretation of rape as intrinsically gender-motivated cannot explain sexual assaults on boys, or the fact that "date rape" is no less common among gay men than among heterosexuals. The statement that "women are raped because they are women" may ring true, but in a biological rather than a political sense: When a man's sexual urges are directed toward women, chances are that his sexual aggression will be too.

Domestic Violence

As for domestic violence, University of British Columbia psychologist Donald Dutton and other researchers have found that wife beating is far more strongly associated with "borderline personality disorder" (characterized by a proclivity for intense relationships, insecurity, and rage) than with patriarchal attitudes; drugs and alcohol are major factors as well. Aside from the much-debated issue of female aggression toward male partners, it is no longer in dispute that physical abuse is at least as common in gay and lesbian couples as in heterosexual ones.

One might point out, too, that male violence is directed mainly at other males. If sexual assault and intimate violence against women are related to gender, surely so are male-on-male attacks triggered by real or perceived slights, sexual rivalry, and thrill seeking. Thugs who rape a woman may also beat up men just for fun, like the teenagers convicted in the notorious 1989 rape of the Central Park jogger. Describing their "wilding" rampage in the park to a detective, one of the teens said that "wilding" meant "going around, punching, hitting on people"—not just women. Yet the attack on the jogger became a paradigm of gender-motivated violence to many feminists; it was cited as such by Helen Neuborne, then president of the National Organization for Women Legal Defense Fund, in testimony to the Senate Judiciary Committee.

Despite these logical flaws, the radical feminist theory of "gender violence" has made significant inroads in the legal system. It was incorporated into the

Violence Against Women Act (VAWA), passed by Congress in 1994, which allows federal civil rights suits for violent crimes "motivated by gender." The application of VAWA, however, is limited by the fact that it provides only for monetary damages. Such litigation, usually lengthy, doesn't make sense unless there are significant assets to go after. Some VAWA cases involve divorcing wives alleging abuse by wealthy husbands; recently, a VAWA lawsuit was filed against basketball bad boy Dennis Rodman by a Las Vegas Hilton casino employee who accuses him of grabbing her by the sides of the torso and lifting her (which, she claims, caused her underwire bra to be painfully pushed into her breast). Other legal action has targeted deep-pocket entities: A suit filed in December 1995 by Christine Brzonkala, a former Virginia Polytechnic student who claimed that she was raped by two male students, named not only the alleged perpetrators but the college as defendants.

> *"Forensic psychology does not support the view that rapists are driven primarily by hatred toward women rather than, say, sexual compulsion or anger at the whole world."*

Double Jeopardy

The Federal Hate Crimes Protection Act, by contrast, would open the door to federal criminal prosecutions for sexual assault or domestic violence, particularly in high-profile cases where an acquittal or dismissal in state courts results in an outcry from women's groups. Men accused of these crimes would effectively lose their double jeopardy protections, like the Los Angeles policemen who were convicted of beating Rodney King. (Under the doctrine of "dual sovereignty," a federal offense is not the same as a state offense, even if it consists of the same action.) However gratifying the outcome of some cases might be, the process is troubling. Moreover, in a "bias" case, the defendant could find himself on trial for having sexist views, watching X-rated movies, or mistreating other women, even if they never went to the police.

Testifying in favor of the expanded federal law in June 1998, Assistant Attorney General Eric Holder reassured the Senate Judiciary Committee that very few "gender-motivated hate crimes" could be prosecuted in federal court, since such prosecutions would require proof of "gender-based bias." But judging from the history of VAWA litigation, which he invoked as a model, the criteria would be elastic enough to apply to any claim of rape or abuse. And that is clearly what the advocates want. At a symposium on VAWA in May 1998, NOW Legal Defense Fund attorney Julie Goldscheid praised the courts for recognizing, "in language that is really heartening to a women's rights advocate, that domestic violence and sexual assault are gender-motivated crimes rooted in the history of discrimination against women."

In Christine Brzonkala's suit against Virginia Polytechnic, the courts found evidence of bias in the fact that the two alleged rapists were virtual strangers to the plaintiff (which should rattle feminist activists who have denounced the notion that acquaintance rape is a lesser crime); that the attack had no motive other than rape; and that, according to Brzonkala, one of the defendants told her, "You'd better not have any fucking diseases." It is worth noting that after hearing the evidence, a Virginia grand jury refused to indict the two men, who claimed that they had consensual sex with Brzonkala—which did not keep her from being invited to the White House Conference on Hate Crimes as a spokeswoman for hate crime victims.

In other cases, federal courts have ruled that alleged acts of sexual violence by themselves justify a claim of gender motivation. In *Jane Doe v. the Rev. Gerald Hartz,* a 1997 case in which an Iowa woman accused her parish priest of kissing and groping her, the court specifically stated that unwanted sexual advances met the gender motivation requirement even if they were "intended to satisfy the actor's sexual desires," since they could also "be demeaning and belittling, and may reasonably be inferred to be intended to have that purpose or to relegate another to an inferior status." In other words, if a priest makes unwanted sexual advances toward a young man, his goal is merely to satisfy his lust, but if he makes unwanted sexual advances toward a young woman, his goal is to relegate her to inferior status. The suit was later thrown out on the grounds that the alleged conduct didn't rise to the level of a violent crime as required by VAWA, but the lower court's interpretation of gender bias went unchallenged.

> *"Many advocates of hate crime laws are less concerned with protecting victims . . . than with making a political point about the pervasiveness of bigotry in American life."*

Two federal courts have given a green light to civil rights suits under VAWA based on allegations of spousal abuse. One case is pending, while the other was settled during the appeals process. Meanwhile, courts in some of the 17 states with hate crime laws that cover gender have applied those statutes in cases of spousal assault. In 1993, a New Hampshire judge used that state's hate crime law in sentencing a man convicted of misdemeanor assault on his girlfriend, after four other women testified that he had abused them while they dated and harassed them after their breakups. There were no allegations that the defendant had ever assaulted any women with whom he was not intimately involved. Such an approach contrasts sharply with the usual analysis of "hate crimes" based on race or ethnicity, where the fact that the victim is selected at random, on the basis of group membership rather than a personal relationship, is considered indicative of bias.

Many advocates of hate crime laws are less concerned with protecting victims or even punishing offenders than with making a political point about the pervasiveness of bigotry in American life. Still, most acts classified as hate crimes probably are based at least partly on actual bigotry. In the case of gender, not only the special treatment of hate crimes but the use of the hate crime label itself—and the analogy with crimes motivated by racial, ethnic, or anti-gay bias—is part of an ideological agenda. The goal is not only to affirm that violence against women is a matter of special concern but that it's part of a male war against women. If no one challenges such ideas in the political arena, it's likely that legislators and judges will continue to give them a seal of approval.

Chapter 2

Should Hate Speech Be Restricted?

Overview: A History of Hate Speech Laws

by Steven J. Heyman

About the author: *Steven J. Heyman, an associate professor of law at Chicago-Kent College of Law, is the editor of the two-volume anthology,* Hate Speech and the Constitution.

> Five high school seniors in Greenwich, Connecticut, insert a coded message into their class yearbook reading "Kill All Niggers."
>
> Berating a worker, an employer repeatedly calls him a "nigger" and tells him that "all you niggers are alike." When the employee objects to the racial slurs and says that he wants to be treated "like a human being," the employer responds, "You're not a human being, you're a nigger."
>
> With a Nazi banner behind him, and surrounded by armed security guards wearing swastikas and SS emblems, the leader of the Aryan World Congress declares at a news conference that Jews are "the bacillus of the decomposition of our society." Escorting them to the conference, an Aryan Nations security guard tells reporters, some of whom he considers nonwhite, "I wish we were marching you into the showers."

In recent years, the United States, like many other democratic nations, has struggled with the problem of hate speech—expression that abuses or degrades others on account of their racial, ethnic, or religious identity. Efforts to regulate such speech have generated a major political and constitutional debate, which has divided many communities and universities, as well as civil libertarians, scholars, and courts. This debate raises crucial issues about the meaning and limits of free expression, and its relationship to other fundamental values such as civility, equality, and dignity.

A Long History

The contemporary controversy over hate speech is so intense that it is easy to forget that the problem is not a recent one, but one with a long history. Indeed,

Excerpted from the Introduction to *Hate Speech and the Constitution: Vol. 1, The Development of the Hate Speech Debate from Group Libel to Campus Speech Codes,* by Steven J. Heyman. Copyright ©1996 by Steven J. Heyman. Reprinted with permission from Taylor & Francis/Routledge, Inc. www.routledge-ny.com.

the problem can be traced back to the first settlement of the country, when it often took the form of conflict between different religious sects. In an early eighteenth century case, the English courts found liability at common law for a false and inflammatory publication that provoked riots against the local Jewish community. Over the following two centuries, English and American courts developed a doctrine of criminal liability for the defamation of groups.

Group Defamation

Responding to interracial conflict and group vilification during the first half of this century, a number of state legislatures enacted criminal laws against group libel. A challenge to the constitutionality of such laws reached the Supreme Court in 1952 in *Beauharnais v. Illinois*. Beauharnais, the leader of a segregationist organization, had distributed a leaflet calling on "one million self respecting white people in Chicago to unite" to "preserve and protect white neighborhoods . . . from the constant and continuous invasion, harassment and encroachment by the negroes." The leaflet added that "[i]f persuasion and the need to prevent the white race from becoming mongrelized by the negro will not unite us, then the aggressions . . . rapes, robberies, knives, guns and marijuana of the negro, surely will."

By a 5 to 4 vote, the Supreme Court upheld Beauharnais's conviction under Illinois' group libel statute, rejecting his contention that the law violated the First Amendment. Justice Felix Frankfurter began his majority opinion by quoting from *Chaplinsky v. New Hampshire*, in which Justice Frank Murphy declared for a unanimous Court:

> There are certain well-defined and narrowly limited classes of speech, the prevention and punishment of which have never been thought to raise any Constitutional problem. These include the lewd and obscene, the profane, the libelous, and the insulting or "fighting" words—those which by their very utterance inflict injury or tend to incite an immediate breach of the peace. It has been well observed that such utterances are no essential part of any exposition of ideas, and are of such slight social value as a step to truth that any benefit that may be derived from them is clearly outweighed by the social interest in order and morality.

If states could constitutionally punish libels against individuals, Justice Frankfurter argued, they could also punish defamation directed at defined groups, so long as there were reasonable grounds for doing so. Reviewing the history of riots and other racial violence in Illinois, Frankfurter found that the legislature could reasonably conclude that "wilful purveyors of falsehood concerning racial and religious groups promote strife and tend powerfully to obstruct the manifold adjustments required for free, ordered life" within a diverse, multiethnic society. Additionally, the legislature could reasonably believe that group defamation diminishes the dignity and opportunities of individuals, whose status in society may be inextricably connected with the reputation of the groups to which they belong. For these reasons, the Court held that group libel laws did not violate the First Amendment.

During the 1960s the Supreme Court greatly expanded its conception of the constitutional guarantees of free speech and press. In the landmark case of *New York Times v. Sullivan*, for example, the Court ruled that libel is not categorically excluded from constitutional protection, and that the First Amendment protects the right of citizens to criticize the conduct of government officials, even if such criticism proves to be inaccurate, as long as it is not knowingly or recklessly false. In subsequent cases, the Court accorded a measure of protection to other forms of defamation as well.

Brandenburg v. Ohio

Free speech doctrine was further extended in *Brandenburg v. Ohio* in 1969. A dozen members of a Ku Klux Klan group led by Brandenburg gathered at a farm to hold a "rally." Wearing Klan regalia and carrying firearms, they burned a large wooden cross. In addition, Brandenburg made a speech threatening that the Klan might have to take "revengence" if the federal government "continues to suppress the white, Caucasian race," and urging that "the nigger should be returned to Africa, the Jew returned to Israel." Films of the rally were made by a local television station crew (who had been invited to attend for this purpose), and were later broadcast both locally and nationally.

> *"Hate speech [is an] expression that abuses or degrades others on account of their racial, ethnic, or religious identity."*

Brandenburg was subsequently convicted of violating Ohio's Criminal Syndicalism statute, which made it an offense to advocate violence or terrorism "as a means of accomplishing industrial or political reform." On appeal, the Supreme Court reversed the conviction, declaring that the First Amendment does not "permit a State to forbid or proscribe advocacy of the use of force or of law violation except where such advocacy is directed to inciting or producing imminent lawless action and is likely to incite or produce such action."

The Nazis in Skokie

Despite the facts of the case, the racist character of the Klan's expression was not an issue in *Brandenburg* (which involved a statute which made no mention of race, but which was enacted around the time of the First World War to combat anarchism). The hate speech issue was raised in the most acute way a decade later, however, when an organization calling itself the National Socialist Party of America (NSPA) announced plans to hold a march in the village of Skokie, Illinois, a Chicago suburb with a large Jewish population, including several thousand survivors of the Nazi Holocaust. The proposed march was to take place for a half-hour in front of the Village Hall, and was to "involve 30 to

50 demonstrators wearing uniforms including swastikas and carrying a party banner with a swastika and placards with statements thereon such as . . . 'Free Speech for White America.'" Skokie officials sought and obtained a preliminary injunction against the march, but the injunction was stayed by the U.S. Supreme Court, and was subsequently reversed by the Illinois courts on First Amendment grounds. In the meantime, the village enacted several ordinances designed to prevent such marches, including one that prohibited the display or distribution of signs, symbols, or other materials that intentionally "promote and incite hatred against persons by reason of their race, national origin, or religion. With the assistance of the American Civil Liberties Union, the NSPA and its leader, Frank Collin, they challenged the ordinances' constitutionality in federal court.

A Violation of the First Amendment

In *Collin v. Smith*, a divided panel of the U.S. Court of Appeals for the Seventh Circuit held that the ordinances violated the First Amendment. The *Chaplinsky* fighting words doctrine could not apply, the court found, because the village did not rely on a fear of responsive violence to justify its position. While acknowledging that the Nazi march would inflict emotional trauma on Holocaust survivors and other Jewish residents, and that this result might indeed be desired by the marchers, the majority ruled that this harm did not justify "engrafting an exception on the First Amendment," for the Nazis' expression was "indistinguishable in principle from speech that 'invite[s] dispute . . . induces a condition of unrest, creates dissatisfaction with conditions as they are, or even stirs people to anger'"—effects that the Supreme Court had previously found to be among the "high purposes" of the First Amendment. To allow the Nazi demonstration to be banned, the court found, would contravene the fundamental principle "'that under our Constitution the public expression of ideas may not be prohibited merely because the ideas are themselves offensive to some of their hearers.'" Village residents could not be considered a captive audience, for they could avoid exposure to the demonstration simply by staying away from the Village Hall while it was taking place. Finally, the Seventh Circuit questioned whether *Beauharnais* remained good law, suggesting that its doctrinal foundations had been undermined by such decisions as *New York Times v. Sullivan*, which

> *"Certain well-defined and narrowly limited classes of speech . . . include the lewd and obscene, the profane, the libelous, and the insulting or 'fighting words.'"*

extended some First Amendment protection to libel, and *Brandenburg*, which narrowed the state's authority to restrict speech because of its tendency to cause violence.

The Supreme Court declined to review the court of appeals' decision. The

Skokie affair and the litigation surrounding it sparked nationwide controversy, and generated a rich and extensive scholarly debate.

Fighting Words

The issue of racist expression most recently confronted the Supreme Court in *R.A.V. v. City of St. Paul*. In that case, the defendant and several other teenagers allegedly burned a crude wooden cross inside the yard of a black family who lived across the street. The defendant was arrested and charged with a violation of a St. Paul ordinance which made it a misdemeanor to "[place] on public or private property a symbol, object, . . . characterization, or graffiti, including, but not limited to, a burning cross or Nazi swastika, which one knows or has reasonable grounds to know arouses anger, alarm or resentment in others on the basis of race, color, creed, religion or gender." The defendant's First Amendment challenge to the ordinance was rejected by the Minnesota Supreme Court, which relied on its own previous decisions interpreting the ordinance narrowly to apply only to expression that amounted to fighting words under *Chaplinsky*.

> *"If states could constitutionally punish libels against individuals, [the Supreme Court argued], they could also punish defamation directed at defined groups."*

The U.S. Supreme Court reversed. Writing for a five-member majority, Justice Antonin Scalia accepted the Minnesota Supreme Court's narrow interpretation of the ordinance. He further assumed, for purposes of argument, that *Chaplinsky's* formulation of the fighting words doctrine remained good law, and that a jurisdiction could therefore prohibit all expressions that inflict injury "by their very utterance . . . or tend to incite an immediate breach of the peace." Nevertheless, Justice Scalia held that the ordinance violated the First Amendment by prohibiting not fighting words in general, but rather only those fighting words that insult or provoke violence on the basis of race, color, creed, religion, or gender. "Selectivity of this sort," Scalia argued, even within a generally unprotected category of speech, "creates the possibility that the city is seeking to handicap the expression of particular ideas" simply because of hostility to them.

The *Skokie* and *R.A.V.* decisions represent the currently prevailing American position on the constitutionality of hate speech regulation, a position which is strongly defended by many liberals and civil libertarians. This position has been subjected to powerful criticism, however, from both the right and the left. For example, a 1974 article by Hadley Arkes advocates reviving the concept of group libel, contending that such expression inflicts injury to its targets and violates the standards of civility and decency requisite for life in a civil society. This argument, which reflects a traditional conservative perspective, draws on *Chaplinsky's* view that certain classes of speech—such as libel, obscenity, and insulting or fighting words—should be unprotected because they contribute little to public debate and undermine "the social interest in order and morality."

The Debate Broadens

During the past decade and a half, this traditional debate between civil libertarians and conservatives has been transformed by the advent of a new perspective on the left that supports hate speech regulation. This view, articulated by the critical race theorists Richard Delgado, Mari Matsuda, and Charles Lawrence and others, advocates restriction of hate speech on the grounds that it inflicts psychological and dignitary injury to its targets, is often connected with violence and intimidation, and reinforces the subordination of historically oppressed groups, thus undermining the principle of equal citizenship expressed in the Fourteenth Amendment. These critics further observe that the prevailing American position on hate speech diverges from that taken by international human rights law and by many other democratic nations, which regard bans on the incitement of racial, ethnic, and religious hatred as necessary for the protection of minorities, and compatible with principles of freedom of expression.

Much of the focus of debate in recent years has been on the regulation of speech on college campuses. Responding to an upsurge in racist incidents, many colleges and universities across the country have adopted policies restricting certain forms of speech. In some cases, these policies have been invalidated under the First Amendment. The validity of many state university policies remains untested, however. Moreover, private institutions are not subject to the First Amendment. Thus, the campus speech debate continues at both public and private universities.

These developments have substantially broadened the traditional debate over the problem of racist speech. They have also produced a realignment within the debate. Thus, many conservatives now join with civil libertarians in opposing hate speech regulations (partly out of concern that they will be used to impose a political orthodoxy), while many progressives support such regulations. At the same time, the political lines have become increasingly blurred. Thus conservatives, liberals, and progressives all find themselves divided over the issue.

> *"Much of the focus of debate in recent years has been on the regulation of speech on college campuses."*

A Central Issue

The hate speech controversy may appear to involve a fundamental conflict between freedom of speech and other important values such as civility and equality. We seem to face a "tragic choice" in which we cannot defend free speech without sacrificing these values, and cannot protect them without doing violence to the ideal of free speech. When confronted with such a choice, it is hardly surprising that we feel torn. The challenge posed by hate speech runs even deeper than this, however, for all of these values are essential to a liberal society. Such a society is founded on principles of equality as well as liberty. Moreover, if a liberal society is to survive, it must be able not only to defend its basic principles, but also to maintain itself as a community. By posing an apparently irreconcilable conflict between liberty, equality, and community, the hate speech problem goes to the core of our political and constitutional order. The participants in the hate speech controversy are right, then, to regard the issue as a central one in constitutional theory.

Some Hate Speech Can Be Restricted

by Margaret Crosby

About the author: *Margaret Crosby, a staff attorney with the American Civil Liberties Union of Northern California, wrote an amicus curiae brief in* Aguilar v. Avis *on behalf of the American Civil Liberties Union of Northern California.*

Editor's Note: On August 2, 1999, in a case known as Aguilar v. Avis, *the California Supreme Court upheld a judge's order prohibiting a supervisor at the Avis Rent-A-Car in San Francisco from using ethnic slurs against Hispanic employees.*

"Man bites dog," media accounts proclaimed, reporting on the American Civil Liberties Union's support of the injunction against workplace racial slurs in *Aguilar v. Avis,* decided by the California Supreme Court on August 2, 1999. That people were surprised by our position is, perhaps, not surprising. The ACLU is identified in the public's mind as the foremost champion of outrageous and offensive speech–flag burning, Nazi marches in Skokie, "indecent" speech on the Internet. We are proud of that tradition, and committed to continuing it.

A Conflict of Rights

But the ACLU protects all fundamental constitutional rights—religious liberty, equality, privacy, and due process, as well as expression. Sometimes speech collides with other cherished rights. When a case involves a conflict of rights, our role is not simply to favor speech over all other fundamental values. Rather, the task of a civil liberties organization, like a court, is to accommodate both rights. This involves evaluating, balancing and ultimately advocating a result that will sacrifice neither fundamental right.

Conflicts of rights have become familiar fare. When do anti-abortion protests invade the privacy rights of clinic staff and patients? When does a student's proselytizing speech violate other students' religious freedom? When do a manager's racist epithets violate the workers' right to racial equality?

In analyzing these questions, we start from several fundamental premises.

Chapter 2

A Right to Be Offensive

First, people have a core right in a free society to be offensive. On the side-walks, they can shout "baby killer" to the woman going to a family planning clinic, "murderer" to the man on trial, "infidel" to the woman of minority faith heading to her place of worship, and any number of racial slurs to people of different races passing by.

We tolerate offensive words, in part because we do not want to give the government power to decide what is good and bad speech, and in part because, in general, we benefit from hearing all views, no matter how provocative. Sometimes, society progresses when we hear speech at the margins—today's heresy may be tomorrow's truth. Sometimes, society progresses when we confront and reject hateful views. Thus, the Constitution's remedy for bad speech is not enforced silence, but more speech.

Second, free speech is not, in the abstract, an enemy of other fundamental values. To the contrary, a robust First Amendment is critical to equality, privacy, religion, and due process.

The civil rights movement's struggle against Jim Crow laws, for example, owes a measure of its success to the Supreme Court's decision constitutionally restricting public official defamation suits. By eliminating the fear of crippling libel judgments from Southern juries, the First Amendment allowed the press to shine a spotlight on the segregated South. The nation saw pictures of "whites only" and "colored" water fountains, and vicious dogs unleashed against peaceful civil rights demonstrators. These vivid images created an unstoppable demand for laws guaranteeing equality.

Similarly, reproductive freedom, the ability of each individual to make child-bearing decisions, depends on access to information. Censorship is a powerful weapon for reproductive rights opponents. Anti-choice governments outlaw birth control information, impose gag rules forbidding doctors at family planning clinics from advising poor women of their right to abortion, ban advertisements for family planning clinics, and strip sex education curricula of contraceptive and safe sex information. In protecting access to health information, the First Amendment protects reproductive choices.

When Rights Collide

Because a weakened First Amendment will ultimately harm not only speech but other fundamental rights, the ACLU disagrees on occasion with our coalition partners and allies when speech conflicts with other rights. Contrary to some organizations dedicated to the separation of church and state, we support the right of private individuals to place religious symbols in public spaces open to other symbolic expression (such as the annual December Menorah in San Francisco's Union Square). We also support student-initiated religious clubs on school campuses that allow other political and social extracurricular student groups. Contrary to some organizations dedicated to defending reproductive rights, we support the right of anti-choice protesters to picket outside of family planning clinics and to march in residential neighborhoods, with gruesome and misleading pictures on their picket signs.

But there comes a point at which conduct undertaken in the name of free speech simply invades other people's fundamental rights.

Sometimes, words are crimes—whether terrorist threats, government bribes or securities frauds. Serious threats of physical harm—as distinct from rhetorical hyperbole—against abortion doctors and their families may be punished. The First Amendment does not compel people to live in fear. Pervasive racial harassment in the workplace—like the barrage of racial slurs cast at Latino workers in the Avis case—is not shielded by the First Amendment.

When an audience is captive, the First Amendment's philosophical assumption that we can avoid or dispute offensive words may not apply. Avis workers could neither avoid nor meaningfully respond to the racist invective their boss cast at them. Students and parents who celebrate their public school graduation need not be the unwilling congregation for a prayer. Doctors, nurses and patients at a family planning clinic need not endure amplified anti-choice slogans broadcast into their health facility all day (although they do need to hear and see this political speech when they walk past the picketers outside).

> *"There comes a point at which conduct undertaken in the name of free speech simply invades other people's fundamental rights."*

True, workers may quit their jobs; parents and students may forego their graduation ceremonies; family planning clinics may shut down—but the First Amendment does not compel that kind of sacrifice to preserve rights of equality, religious freedom, or privacy. In these situations, the courts may prevent the racial harasser, the religious proselytizer, and the anti-choice bullhorn broadcaster from violating other people's fundamental right not to listen to their message.

A Delicate Task

Even in these situations, limiting speech is a task of great delicacy. Courts are called upon to craft orders with pinpoint precision. They must act only after full and fair fact-finding, and they must restrict the least amount of expressive activity, barring only the behavior that directly invades other fundamental rights.

In the Avis case, for example, the court issued its injunction only after a jury awarded damages based on the supervisor's repeatedly hurling racist epithets at his Latino employees (a conclusion which Avis did not challenge, thereby conceding that the speech was not constitutionally protected). The court further found, based on the trial testimony, that the manager would persist in continuing his racial harassment once he left the courthouse. The Supreme Court upheld a narrow injunction, which halts only the conduct found to be unlawful.

The order is limited to the harasser, bars him only from spewing racist slurs at the Avis facility, and most importantly, prevents him from casting only "derogatory racial or ethnic epithets directed at or descriptive of" Latino employees at Avis, victims of his prior discrimination.

The Avis order is a modest effort to secure equality for Latino workers who have suffered race discrimination. And freedom of speech, including offensive speech, remains robust. The Avis supervisor retains his right to step outside and give voice to his bigoted views. He may walk down the street, hurling racial slurs at passing strangers—who, unlike his employees, may give him a vigorous response.

Complex, contemporary California society presents numerous conflicts of rights situations. When fundamental rights collide, courts are obligated to explore every method of accommodating conflicting values. Few tasks are more sensitive, more difficult, or more important. As an organization dedicated to protecting the civil liberties of all people, we, too, welcome the challenge.

The Case for Campus Speech Codes

by Richard Delgado

About the author: *Richard Delgado, the Jean Lindsley Professor of Law at the University of Colorado at Boulder, is the coauthor of* Must We Defend Nazis? Hate Speech, Pornography, and the New First Amendment, *and* The Price We Pay: The Case Against Racist Speech, Hate Propaganda, and Pornography.

In this viewpoint, I first address [the] central premise about governmental control of speech. Then, I address some subordinate issues about hate-speech regulation: [the] contention that minorities have no business writing about hate speech because we are blinded by self-interest, for example. Finally, I offer a perspective for understanding social resistance . . . to reform in this area.

The Role of Government

[It is pointed] out that anti-hate-speech activists have dishonorable predecessors in Supreme Court Justices who approved suppression of political speech.

But, of course, [the] heroes have their blind spots, too: Thomas Hobbes and John Locke wrote approvingly of slavery, and Supreme Court Justice Oliver Wendell Holmes wrote *Buck v. Bell* [which approved involuntary sterilization of Carrie Lee Buck, who was supposedly mentally retarded, on the theory that "three generations of imbeciles are enough"] and was a camp follower of the American eugenics movement that advocated restrictions on the immigration of persons of color and controls on breeding of groups deemed inferior.

And, as everyone knows, the First Amendment coexisted with slavery for nearly one hundred years.

Is it a standoff, then—one side's favorite value and stock interpretation of history pitted against another's? I do not believe so, for [the] characterization of the other side contains a glaring flaw: Controlling hate speech differs radically from controlling the speech of a political dissident.

Consider an analogy from a related area, social and political satire. The classic writers in this genre, such as Jonathan Swift, Voltaire, and Mark Twain, re-

Excerpted from "Are Hate-Speech Rules Constitutional Heresy? A Reply to Steven Gey," by Richard Delgado, *University of Pennsylvania Law Review,* March 1998. Reprinted with permission.

served their barbs for the wealthy and powerful kings and other governmental figures who abused power, the idle rich, or the complacent bourgeoisie.

They scrupulously avoided making fun at the expense of the poor or the crippled, but instead tweaked pomposity and self-importance among the ruling class.

As Jean Stefancic and I wrote in the *William and Mary Law Review*, "A root meaning of 'humor' is humus—bringing low, down to earth. . . ." Clearly, deflating a government bureaucrat or a puffed-up rich person stands on different footing from poking fun at someone who is poor or afflicted with a disease.

A similar intuition applies to censorship. Suppression of speech is odious when it is government that is censoring the speech of a weak, voiceless dissident.

There, the dangers of silencing, governmental self-aggrandizement, and nest-feathering rise to their most acute level. A powerful actor like government should never be above criticism. But with hate-speech regulation, the opposite situation prevails—an arm of government, usually a university, is intervening to prevent private harm.

Far from trying to insulate itself from criticism, or intervening on the side of the powerful, the university is acting on behalf of persons who are disempowered vis-a-vis their tormentors. Because few, if any, of the dangers of censorship loom, it seems perverse to use the term in that way, just as it would sound strange to call a story ridiculing blind people satire.

[Critics are] particularly concerned with the social-construction justification for anti-hate-speech measures.

Justification

I think it perfectly sensible—who would want to live in a society ten or twenty percent of whose members were regularly demeaned by face-to-face insults and in popular culture? But even if not, this is by no means the only interest proregulation writers have advanced. Racist speech damages the dignity, pecuniary prospects, and psyches of its victims (particularly children), while it impedes the ability of colleges to diversify their student bodies.

When severe or protracted, it can even cause physical sickness, including high blood pressure, tremors, sleep disturbance, and early death.

In focusing only on the most abstract and novel of the justifications, . . . overlooked [is the fact] that hate-speech rules are necessary to promote a number of social and educa-

> *"Controlling hate speech differs radically from controlling the speech of a political dissident."*

tional objectives of a quite ordinary nature. Moreover, [critics] often blithely [invoke] the informed social consensus or "common understanding" as though these were not social constructs, and [ignore] that the status quo (in which minorities suffer frequent slights and insults) has a bias, too.

Social constructionism, it turns out, is impermissible only when wielded by minorities seeking to change the prevailing situation.

In addition, in [the] fixation on the supposed political dangers of hate-speech regulation, . . . the numerous other "exceptions" and special doctrines that riddle free-speech law [are overlooked]—libel, defamation (even of vegetables and produce), words of threat and of monopoly, state secrets, copyright, plagiarism, disrespectful speech uttered to a judge or other authority figure, and many more.

> *"Who would want to live in a society ten or twenty percent of whose members were regularly demeaned by face-to-face insults and in popular culture?"*

With these, the state intervenes on behalf of actors who are quite empowered, such as the military, agribusiness, or the community of commercially successful authors, and where the risks of aggrandizement and increase of power are very real. Government, authors, consumers, and other powerful groups are able to suppress speech that offends them, but when a university proposes a speech code to protect some of the most defenseless members of society—black, brown, gay, or lesbian undergraduates at dominantly white institutions—[we are charged] with constitutional heresy and warn[ed] that we will all end up thought-controlled zombies.

But racism is a classic case of democratic failure; to insist that minorities be at the mercy of private remonstrance against their tormentors—and that the alternative is censorship—is to turn things on their head. . . .

Other Pieces of the Picture

Other charges [are leveled] against the hate-speech camp. As minorities in most (but not all) cases, we are apt to be partial—too close to the problem to write about it objectively.

But then why is . . . a white male not similarly disqualified from taking the contrary position? Readers are of course capable of evaluating for themselves an argument made by a minority, just as they are one by [a white male] but [this] oversight of the way that [this] argument cuts both ways is telling. An example of white transparency, it shows how the white point of view masquerades as colorless, raceless, and systematically devoid of bias.

[This] argument not only ignores much recent scholarship, but also would disqualify consumers from arguing for consumer protection laws, medical patients from urging changes in medical malpractice law, and anyone else with an interest in a controversy from writing about it—clearly not a position we take in general.

[Another argument is] that everyone has the right to be obnoxious and wrong.

But this certainly is not true—we regulate many forms of obnoxiousness, and should.

Nor do anti-hate-speech advocates argue for regulation of hate speech because it is wrong in any factual sense. The campus tough who snarls, "Nigger, go back to Africa. You don't belong on this campus," is not conveying information. The victim already knows that he is an African-American, that the speaker and many others do not like him or welcome his presence on campus, and that his ancestors came from Africa. Face-to-face hate speech conveys no information. It is more like a slap in the face or a performative (like "You're on," or, "I now pronounce you man and wife"); it reorders the speaker's and the listener's statuses in relation to each other.

Indeed, regulating these stunning transactions might well result in more speech on campus, not less. Feeling more welcome and less beleaguered, students of color would be more likely to speak out and participate more actively in classroom discussions.

[Some critics reason] that hate-speech rules are unnecessary because the numerous civil rights acts passed since 1957 are very broad-reaching.

But useful as that landmark legislation may be, it certainly has not been fully successful. Recent studies by "testers," one black, one white, but otherwise as alike as possible, show the radically different receptions they receive when shopping, renting an apartment, buying a car, or applying for a loan or job.

Today, more African-American children attend segregated schools than did in [1954].

And even if these more tangible forms of discrimination were on the wane, hate-speech rules would still be necessary to counter a cultural legacy of racism and pernicious stereotypes. [One critic] warns that this would be tantamount to brainwashing and thought control, but he overlooks that society already employs a variety of means to discourage racism, including education, laws, and official statements.

Hate-speech rules would be no more intrusive than many of these measures.

The Slippery-Slope Argument

Finally, what are we to make of [the] repeated deployment of the shopworn slippery-slope argument that if courts give government the power to regulate speech in one area, it will soon seize even more and use it in ways minorities might not like? One notices immediately that . . . this argument [is made] almost entirely by means of hypothetical language: Once courts give the go-ahead to hate-speech rules, other branches of government "may," "could," "could easily," or "undoubtedly would" pass laws punishing speech we prize, including (possibly, maybe, likely) even anti-racist speech itself.

Anything is possible, of course, but it just has not happened. Colleges that have enacted anti-hate-speech rules have not proceeded ineluctably to enact even more sweeping rules or put everyone in jail.

Western democracies that have enacted hate-speech laws, such as Canada, Denmark, France, Germany, and the Netherlands, have scarcely suffered a diminution of respect for free speech.

The few examples [critics do] give of speech suppression, mainly McCarthy-era witch hunts, took place long before hate-speech rules were in effect and were more the product of political excess than lack of First Amendment zeal.

Indeed, during the McCarthy hearings, the nation's leading First Amendment organization, the American Civil Liberties Union (ACLU), chose to lay low instead of forcefully confronting McCarthyism and blacklists.

A second example of censorship, . . . from Canada, has been refuted by later investigation.

Not only does First Amendment absolutism offer little bulwark against governmental repression, it has provided less help than is commonly supposed for minorities in their struggle against racism. Despite the frequent admonition that minorities, if they knew their own best interest, would not limit the First Amendment, civil rights reformers have made the greatest progress when they acted against the First Amendment, at least as it was then understood.

Speech may have served as a useful vehicle for racial reform, but the system of free speech generally did not.

Who Is in Charge?

Note how [critics write] as though minorities were now in charge and running things. When conditions change, [they warn], the new regime may use hate-speech rules and the new regulatory power against the very people who advocated them.

But to argue that minorities are running the show now—when the political right is ascendant, rolling back affirmative action, curtailing immigration and the language rights of non-English speakers . . . and dismantling campus programs that differ even slightly from the Western canon—is ludicrous.

In reality, it is our very powerlessness and vulnerability that cause a few universities to consider passing hate-speech rules. Note as well how . . . First Amendment absolutists, [ignore] that slopes are arguably just as slippery in the other direction. I might just as easily argue that failure to regulate hate speech, thereby leaving an important aspect of equality unprotected, could lead to further erosion.

"Hate speech rules would still be necessary to counter a cultural legacy of racism and pernicious stereotypes."

Racists could become emboldened, and who knows what the next outrage might be? . . .

Perverse Neutralism

How could simple antiracist measures aimed at advancing the civil rights agenda seem like tyranny and thought control?

In some respects, the hate-speech controversy is the *Plessy v. Ferguson* of our age. In that case, a railroad passenger challenged a Louisiana statute that forced blacks to ride in one railroad car while whites rode in another.

The Supreme Court upheld this official system. Each group was legally disadvantaged. Neither could ride in the cars set aside for the other: separate but equal.

Almost sixty years later, *Brown v. Board of Education* overruled *Plessy,* finding that separate schools harmed black children irreparably, in violation of the Fourteenth Amendment's guarantee of equal protection.

Shortly after the *Brown* decision was announced, a well-known constitutional scholar asked how the opinion could be justified on neutral grounds.

To the scholar, it seemed to sacrifice the right of whites not to associate with blacks to that of blacks to do the converse. Why is the one right more deserving of respect than the other?

In the hate-speech debate, we see much the same sort of perverse neutralism. The white . . . insists on the freedom to say whatever is on his mind. The black or brown insists on the right not to hear what is on the white's mind when that takes the form of a vicious racial slur. One interest balanced against another, one emanating from one part of the Constitution (the First Amendment), the other from a different part (the Fourteenth Amendment)—seemingly a perfect standoff. As with *Plessy,* I think history will have no trouble telling us which interest is more morally significant.

Hate Speech Must Be Condemned

by Sanford Cloud Jr.

About the author: *Sanford Cloud Jr. is the president and chief executive officer of the National Conference for Community and Justice, formerly known as the National Conference of Christians and Jews, an organization dedicated to fighting prejudice and racism.*

Appealing to hate, especially in times of economic insecurity, is a time-tested insidious tactic increasingly being mainstreamed in modern American dialogue. Joe McCarthy did it, to serious effect. The Neo-Nazis and white supremacists do it—witness the Montana Freemen. Certain religious leaders do it, and gain media attention. And, recently, some of our politicians have done it. This effective technique drives wedges between fellow workers and neighbors, and alienates us from people we do not even know. At worst, it inspires hatred and violence.

The Modus Operandi

The modus operandi involves a leader appealing to segments of the population whose sense of self is shaky, often due to tough economic times. Corporate downsizing, restructuring, re-engineering, rising costs, diminishing quality of life and the threat of lost jobs stir anxieties. People fear that they won't be able to care for their families.

Recognizing this as a fertile breeding ground, a leader steps to the podium and rallies the fearful and angry by blaming their troubles squarely or implicitly on some "other" ethnic, racial, socioeconomic or religious group. The leader then positions himself as the brave spokesperson of "truth," who will challenge the enemy—the "other"—who has caused the problem. With someone to look down upon, the fearful feel empowered and define themselves as members of a superior group, more valuable than those "others."

Historically, specific ethnic, racial, political and religious groups have been targeted as the threat. For Hitler, it was Jews, Catholics, gypsies and homosexuals. Joe McCarthy's enemies were liberals, in particular, members of the Holly-

Reprinted with permission from "The People Shouldn't Be Swayed by Appeals to Hatred," by Sanford Cloud Jr., *People's Weekly World*, September 7, 1996.

wood community. Today, some members of that same entertainment community are maligning the Jews, while films stereotype people of color as violent youths.

The Klan burns its crosses and Moslems are attacked as the purveyors of terrorism, while some African American leaders rail against white America. The Montana Freemen defrauded the financial community as a statement against our government and in furtherance of their view that white male Christians are the sole intended beneficiaries of the U.S. Constitution. For each, the message is the same: silence, stop or eliminate the "other" and you—the unfairly victimized—will triumph.

Wedge Issues

It is relatively easy to recognize the appeal-to-hate tactic in its extreme forms. But today, the tactic is becoming ever more subtle, as leaders begin to use wedge issues that are silent synonyms for targeted groups. Through insinuation, allusion and even clear statements, certain leaders, a number of elected officials and some who would have been president, have fanned the flames of hate, by using wedge issues—such as immigration, welfare and affirmative action—to divide. Creating a "them" versus "us," either/or mentality through appeals to fear, these leaders have offered simple, palatable explanations to the complex social, economic and political changes rocking Americans today.

Regarding immigration, for example, we've recently heard talk about constructing walls at our borders and, alternatively, about a new branch of the armed forces to keep out illegal immigrants. Here, the wedge argument is simple: The real Americans must stop the immigrants who are

> *"If we do not [condemn hate speech], we will have endorsed through silence a climate that sanctions the language of hate, [and] permits bias crimes."*

taking the jobs of U.S. citizens, adding to crime, destroying our communities or, when they are not working, living off welfare. Forget that immigrants take low-paying jobs that others will not accept, that some clean the hotel rooms where presidential candidates stay and that they pay taxes. Forget that they enrich our culture. Forget that America is, after all, a country of immigrants save for Native Americans. And forget to differentiate between illegal immigrants and those who legally come with special skills or to join family members. But, most of all, forget that the current arguments are not new. Almost 100 years ago they were hurled at Irish, Jewish and other Central European emigres.

With welfare, those who breed division play on the commonly held assumptions that most welfare recipients are African American or Hispanic, have a large number of children to increase their checks, regularly double their benefits through fraud, and readily stay on welfare for the long haul because they do not want to work. Each of these beliefs is untrue. But many hardworking, taxpaying Americans believe them and are angry at those in need of help. To many, welfare reform now means eliminating support totally, rather than seeking a creative and considered response toward those who can achieve self-support and those who might starve without our help.

Insidious and Dangerous

While people of good will may recognize and condemn overt appeals to hate, they too often dismiss the use of the more subtle wedge arguments. But this method of gaining public attention, relying as it does on fear and hatred, is insidious and dangerous. It dehumanizes whole groups and, in so doing, obfuscates complex issues so that realistic but humane solutions are left outside of the national debate.

It is time for us to take stock and call upon leaders in all walks of life and, in particular, the presidential candidates who will receive so much media attention, to meet their obligation to sharply, openly and honestly debate issues and avoid taking America down the path toward division and suspicion.

We must remain mindful that, while the U.S. Constitution properly protects free speech, history shows that the rhetoric that preys on insecurities breeds a milieu receptive to hatred of some "other." Americans can and should tolerate all points of view, even when distasteful. What we must not tolerate is the silence of people of good will, who by their passivity allow the noxious use of wedge issues to be mainstreamed, creating a vacuum into which the venom of hate is welcome. We must join our voices, speak loudly, clearly and in a civil manner against this tactic. We must respond with facts to those who would appeal to the worst in us. And we must expressly condemn the conduct of those who would use direct or implied scapegoating as a tool for gaining public attention, power or election. If we do not, we will have endorsed through silence a climate that sanctions the language of hate, permits bias crimes and perhaps, ultimately, crates random acts of group violence throughout our nation.

Hate Speech Should Not Be Restricted

by Paul K. McMasters

About the author: *Paul K. McMasters is the First Amendment ombudsman at the Freedom Forum, a foundation that focuses on speech and press issues.*

More than one year has passed, and we have yet to shake the image of Matthew Shepard pistol-whipped and strung up to die on a Wyoming rail fence in October 1998 because he was gay. We still shudder over the horror of James Byrd chained to a pickup truck and dragged to his death along a Texas country road in June 1998 because he was black. We cringe when reminded of the racist rampage of Benjamin Smith that left two people dead and nine others wounded in July 1999.

America, we like to feel, has room for everyone. It is a place of tolerance, equality, and justice. Hate is a singular affront to that vision, and the lengthening list of these atrocities haunts the national conscience and quickens the search for a remedy.

It once seemed easier to ignore the haters among us. They held furtive meetings in out-of-the-way places, wrote racist screeds in the guise of bad novels, and when they appeared in public, they wore hoods to hide their faces. Now, they apply for admission to the bar, stand for elected office, appear on radio and television talk shows, and increasingly take their message to the mainstream by using the Internet.

Hate has been a presence on the Internet since its inception. That presence increased dramatically with the advent of the World Wide Web. Now such sites, professionally produced and graphically appealing, number in the hundreds. More go up every day. Activists have moved quickly to confront the haters on this virtual ground, using the Internet to give the lie to hate speech, to monitor hate groups, and to highlight the problems of hate.

Thus, the Internet is forcing us to plumb the true depth of hate in our society. Because the role the Internet will play in the matter of hate is still evolving, the

Reprinted with permission from "Must a Civil Society Be a Censored Society?" by Paul K. McMasters, *Human Rights,* Fall 1999.

question arises: Will the Internet prove to be an instrument of hate, a palliative to hate, or just a shift in venue? The answer will depend in large measure on the nature of the solutions to hate that we pursue.

Hate Speech

Among the proposals advanced are restrictions on hate speech. Generally, hate speech is that which offends, threatens, or insults groups based on race, color, religion, national origin, gender, sexual orientation, disability, or a number of other traits. Proposals to restrict such speech have considerable support among victim groups, civil rights activists, scholars, political figures, and ordinary citizens. The arguments for restrictions on hate speech, whether on the Internet or elsewhere, are straightforward: Words can and do harm the targets of hate in painfully real ways; hate speech silences the members of victim groups and denies them their rightful standing in society; there already are exceptions to First Amendment protections for other types of speech—surely hate speech can be added to that list; when it comes to hate speech, civil rights must trump civil liberties.

The calls for restrictions include declaring hate mongers mentally ill, government monitoring of groups and individuals espousing hate, outright censorship of hate speech on the Internet, and punishment of hate

> *"There is another, more difficult, problem for the advocates of [hate speech] laws: they don't stop hate."*

speech in all forms and media. It has even been proposed that recent hate outrages justify lifting the restraints placed on the Hoover-era Federal Bureau of Investigation to allow the agency to investigate groups and individuals for religious or political speech it deems extreme.

Most Americans want to do something about the hate. In the aftermath of the October 1998, beating death of Matthew Shepard, the University of Wyoming student targeted because he was gay, twenty-six states took up legislative proposals dealing with hate crimes. Missouri passed such a law, and California Governor Gray Davis signed a bill that outlaws harassment of gays in state schools.

The Debate

It is a uniquely American characteristic that such matters become the stuff of passionate debate rather than bloody warfare—remarkable considering the seriousness and divisiveness of the issues raised. When laws target speech, whether on the Internet or in other venues, profound questions are raised. Do group sensibilities take precedence over individual conscience? Is some speech so odious and hurtful that it can be regarded as conduct? Must the achievement of a civil society be at the expense of a free society?

However we eventually resolve such questions, the debate must play out in terms of what the Constitution will allow. The Supreme Court has been wary of a general proscription of hate speech. Beginning with *Cantwell v. Connecticut,* (1940), the Court set about defining and refining the conditions under which hate speech might fall outside the First Amendment's protections. A series of these decisions—*Chaplinsky v. New Hampshire,* (1942); *Terminiello v. Chicago,* (1949); *Feiner v. New York,* (1951); and *Brandenburg v. Ohio,* (1969)—have added such terms as "clear and present danger," "fighting words," "incitement to . . . imminent lawless action," and "the heckler's veto" to the legal lexicon. Even so,

> *"It does not necessarily follow that hate speech causes either hate crimes or the silencing of victim groups or that anti-hate speech laws will relieve either problem."*

no ruling has yet yielded up a "victim's veto." With the unanimous decision in *R.A.V. v. St. Paul,* (1992), which held that a bias-motivated criminal ordinance was invalid because it prohibited "otherwise permitted speech solely on the basis of the subjects the speech addresse[d]," that seems even less likely today.

In addition, there are other constitutional obstacles such as the jurisprudence involving prior restraint, group libel, and the right to private conscience (an issue explored at some length by Alan Charles Kors and Harvey A. Silverglate in *The Shadow University: The Betrayal of Liberty on America's Campuses*). Nevertheless, judges and juries in state courts are listening intently to efforts to make the case against hate speech. Attempts to expand the concepts of threat or the intentional infliction of emotional distress offer hope to advocates that a constitutionally valid approach can be devised.

Even if laws that the Supreme Court would abide could be crafted, however, there is another, more difficult, problem for the advocates of such laws: they don't stop hate. That is the fundamental flaw in solutions that focus on hate speech laws. The proponents of such laws frequently fail to disentangle three distinct issues: hate speech, hate crimes, and the silencing of victim groups. Hate causes each of these. It does not necessarily follow that hate speech causes either hate crimes or the silencing of victim groups or that anti-hate speech laws will relieve either problem. Censoring hate speech may have emotional and symbolic appeal but little if any utility as a solution.

Outside the United States, hate often manifests itself in prolonged and violent clashes between groups. International conventions and anti-hate speech laws don't seem to have had an appreciable impact on hate or the violence that it causes, however. We have had the same experience with campus speech codes in the United States. Not only have they not found much favor with the courts; more importantly, hate speech and crimes on the nation's campuses have increased appreciably despite the existence of speech codes covering broad categories of speech at hundreds of colleges and universities. In fact, women and minorities—traditional groups for whom the speech codes were enacted—often are the ones punished under them. It is instructive to note that the defendants in the early hate speech cases were religious or political speakers. In *Cantwell* and *Chaplinsky,* they were Jehovah's Witnesses, in *Terminiello,* a Catholic priest (albeit under suspension from his bishop at the time for racist speech), and in *Feiner,* a college student appealing to blacks to resist racist oppression.

Defining Hate Speech

The difficulty of defining hate speech significantly complicates attempts to draft laws against hate speech. What might work for scholarly or general discourse surely would not be adequate for the formulation of laws. Is the definition in terms of what the speech reflects, such as bigotry, bias, prejudice, anger, ignorance, and fear? Or what the speech conveys: intimidation, vilification, subjugation, eradication? Does it matter whether the speech occurs in a face-to-face encounter, in an online diatribe, in a novel, in a newscast, during a classroom presentation, or as part of a political candidate's campaign? Can hate speech be defined as a list of words, or does the context of those words count? Which is more important in determining hate speech, the intent of the speaker or the reaction of the audience?

Once a definition of hate speech is codified in law, the problem becomes one of determining how it is applied and to whom it is applied. Should a law proscribe certain words and thoughts for one group of Americans but allow them for oppressed groups that have appropriated the language of victimization and discrimination as a strategy for combating hate?

For hate laws to function, hate groups must be designated for special punishment of their words and views, and victim groups must be designated for special consideration—a seductive prospect in light of their history of oppression. Ultimately, however, it is an inconsistent and possibly disastrous principle to embed in law, given the potential for arbitrary justice as well as a hardening of the hate lines. Further, to punish hatemongers for thoughts and words instead of actions is to alter the essential nature of our social and political compact.

> *"To punish hatemongers for thoughts and words instead of actions is to alter the essential nature of our social and political compact."*

The Problem with Hate Speech Laws

Hate speech laws encourage appropriation of victim groups' identities by groups that until recently had not been considered oppressed. The list of such "outsider" groups is growing. For example, an Oregon law includes along with the traditional criteria such designations as political party, purchasing power, union membership, social standing, or marital status, to name a few. As this list of victim groups expands, the universe of protected speech shrinks.

Hate speech laws can work to silence individual members of victim groups if the speech against others falls within the definition of hate speech or if individuals within the group are only allowed to represent that group in their speech. They would be prevented from criticizing or harshly characterizing members of their own group or other victim groups.

Hate speech laws also must depend on an accurate representation of how speech works, reasonably predicting how speech will be received. If not, application of the law becomes arbitrary and capricious. For example, if inadvertent harm is a criterion of the law—and how could it not be?—then speech against hate as well as hate speech itself becomes vulnerable to punishment since inadvertent harm is inevitable. The ironic beauty of speech is that neither the speaker nor the text can control the reaction of the audience, which may vary dramatically from one hearer to another. It is safe to say that the interpretations of a particular word or string of words in a particular context amount to some multiple of the total number of individuals and groups receiving it. Language is simply too mercurial for the constraints of legal definitions.

> *"Punishing speech is not the same thing as curing hate."*

Laws against hate speech would obviate the benefits of such speech—and there are benefits. Hate speech uncovers the haters. It exposes the ignorance, fear, and incoherence in their views. It warns, prepares, and galvanizes the targets. It provides the police with suspects and the prosecutors with evidence in the event of a crime. It enlivens the bystanders. It demands response. And it demonstrates the strength of our commitment to the tolerance of intolerance and the primacy of freedom of expression.

Laws restricting hate speech begin with the assumption that speech is a finite commodity, so that speech must be taken from one group in order to give more speech to another group. Such an assumption offends both reason and our First Amendment tradition.

Punishing speech is not the same thing as curing hate. Ultimately, anti–hate speech laws would silence the voices they would help as well as those who would help them. They would be enacted with the best of intentions and executed with the worst of results. Rather than encouraging the assimilation of the words and work of those championing a more civil society, these laws would substitute one form of silencing for another. They would divert public dialogue from a focus on a fair society to a preoccupation with censorship. They would risk exacerbating hate rather than eliminating it. They would trivialize the debate by flailing at words and symbols rather than the causes of hate and discrimination. They would lay a veneer of civility over a community seething with tension.

Even though arguments against hate speech laws from a First Amendment perspective seem anemic and abstract in the face of hate's graphic ugliness, they must be made. Free speech advocates cannot merely wave the First Amendment flag and walk away. They must encourage advocates for the targets of hate to speak out against bigotry and bias at every turn. They must remind them that protecting and exercising the freedom guaranteed under the First Amendment is the best way to insure the equality guaranteed under the Fourteenth Amendment.

All efforts must focus on affirming the American tradition that no problem—even hate—is so intractable that we must censor words, images, and ideas to address it. The challenge within that tradition is to achieve civility in discourse without imposing conformity in thought. The First Amendment imperative within that tradition is to defend bad words for good principles.

The Case Against Campus Speech Codes

by Stephen A. Smith

About the author: *Stephen A. Smith is a professor of communication at the University of Arkansas.*

My position and my argument is not only that hate speech codes are patently unconstitutional under the First Amendment, it is also that they are a bad idea as a matter of public policy. When first asked to contribute to this collection of essays, I suggested that the editors might wish to enlist someone else to write about hate speech, because I am, in a sense, for it. But, let me explain that statement.

Speech Codes Do Not Change Beliefs

The corrosive emotion of hate is, I think, a manifestation of the emotion of fear, created by economic insecurity, relative status deprivation, lack of education, feelings of powerlessness, sexual insecurity, or a more general fear of all differences as disconfirming the validity of one's own personal security. The expression of these feelings and targeting them toward some "other" is, I think, what concerns the advocates of hate speech codes. Even if these codes were constitutional, they cannot be effective. Proscribing the words does nothing to change the underlying thoughts and fears; hate speech does not express the unthinkable, only the unreasonable. In fact, suppression of speech often exacerbates and intensifies the sentiments of those silenced by law, while denying to everyone the opportunity to seek and discover wisdom through debate and the clash of ideas. On the other hand, a convincing case can be made that fostering freedom of speech can result in greater tolerance among citizens with differing views.

Hate speech is much like a canker sore on the body politic. Legal restrictions on hate speech only suppress the symptoms; they do not treat the underlying causes of the social disease. Applying the Band-Aid of a speech code might keep it from the sight of those who would be repulsed, but the infection would remain and fester. A better prescription would be to expose it to the air of speech and the light of reason, the healing antibiotic of counterargument.

Furthermore, hate speech can serve an important social and political function. Irrational expressions of hate based on the status of the targets can alert us to the fact that something is wrong—in the body politic, in ourselves, or in the speakers. It might suggest that some change is necessary, or it might only warn us against the potential for demagogues. Speech codes, ordinances, and statutes would (if they could be enforced) blind us to the problems and deny us the opportunity to solve them before they broke out into actions.

> *"Hate speech codes are patently unconstitutional under the First Amendment."*

Senator Frank Lautenberg, in a Senate speech condemning the remarks of Khalid Abdul Muhammad and recognizing that the message was protected by the First Amendment, made the point quite eloquently:

> We condemn Mr. Muhammad and his message. [Khalid Muhammad is a former spokesman for the Nation of Islam who gave an anti-Semitic, antiwhite, anti-Catholic, antigay speech at Kean College in New Jersey in 1994.] But we must also reach out to the students who were moved by his rhetoric of hate and attracted by his words of violence.
>
> Mr. President, we must figure out why those words fall on receptive ears. We have to come to grips with the fact that some of our students liked what they heard.
>
> Why? Why did they like what they heard? The answer is they are like other people—capable of prejudice. The answer is that the poverty, the racism, the hopelessness, they have witnessed in their communities has stoked anger—and it is a small step from anger to hatred. The answer is that many have been treated badly—and feel the system leaves them out. The answer is that they have seen racist statements made by whites—prominent whites in some cases—go unchallenged.
>
> Mr. President, we need to condemn what was said in the strongest possible terms. But, in the end, we have to do more than condemn. We have to respond so that we prevent prejudice from taking seed and growing and bursting into a deadly bloom.
>
> We have not found a way to reach the students who cheered Mr. Muhammad's speech. We have not been successful in dealing with their pain and their anger—which can easily spill over to violent episodes of rage and hatred.
>
> That, Mr. President, is the hard part of what we have to do.

Hate speech codes might have other negative effects as well; they might actually inhibit, rather than enhance, the education of students and the development of responsible citizens. Republican theory has long recognized that active citizenship is hard work, that tumults are often the price of liberty in self-governing republics, that tumultuous liberty was preferable to ordered despotism, and that good laws were of no avail if the people were corrupt. The same rationale might be applied to analyzing the relationship between free speech and speech codes as they relate to the goals of the university and the realities of racism.

Speech Codes Are Easier than Changing Attitudes

Adopting hate speech codes is much easier than working to change the attitudes that lead to their consideration. As one study concluded, university

> administrators must weigh the value of punishing hate speech against the fundamental educational mission. Educating those who verbally abuse others requires a greater commitment of time, energy, and resources than does punishing such offenders. But the ultimate effect more nearly meets the goal of higher education: to expand the mind and heart beyond the fear of the unknown, opening them to the whole range of human experiences.

Blenda Wilson, President of Cal State-Northridge, seemed to express such an understanding and make that choice. In describing the approach on her campus, she said,

> What happens here is not only that there's tension but that it's a tension that as a university community we are charged to understand, to articulate, to respond to. We have a responsibility as a university not only to educate people in terms of knowledge, but to help create future citizens.
>
> It would be inappropriate and wrong for a university and community to purport to be a homogeneous community in which there is no tension over ideas. So we don't back away from it in the ways that genteel society avoids these kinds of tensions. And more than that, we have young people, so we have emotions involved. We have deep feelings of growing up and maturing and what that means.
>
> These will be the leaders and the citizens and the employees in a multiethnic, multicultural society. If we can provide a place where the tensions that come out of our past are understood better, then our graduates indeed will be able to lead in a moral and tolerant way.

First Amendment Protection

In conclusion, I argue unapologetically here for First Amendment protection for hate speech and against constitutionally unwarranted codes that only hide the symptoms of such social maladies. The solution I suggest is something much more difficult. It demands listening carefully, thinking rationally, judging critically, and refuting vigorously those ideas and ideologies we find offensive or wrong. Such an approach requires both skill and courage, but

> *"Proscribing the words does nothing to change the underlying thoughts and fears."*

the *res publica* will benefit most from allowing such expression and by a public refutation showing it to be wrong. Even those who accept the communitarian diagnosis of the ills of contemporary society, do not advocate unconstitutional speech codes but recognize individual rights and stress the responsibility to exercise moral suasion urging the rejection of unacceptable ideas.

In a thoughtful analysis of the costs and benefits of freedom of speech, Simon Lee noted, and I agree, that free speech controversies are almost always high constitutional moments or important episodes in our personal lives. They should make us aware not only of the free speech issues but of deeper cultural issues demanding attention. We might, he contends, facilitate better solutions to both sides of the conflict if we can strengthen broad public support for the free flow and critical reception of ideas. To make speech more valuable we should work to foster a society in which more people have the ability to analyze information and opinion critically, where minority groups and the minority have the self-confidence that comes from being respected and accepted, where tolerance is a general virtue, where people can reflect and argue, speaking rather than shouting.

> *"Irrational expressions of hate based on the status of the targets can alert us to the fact that something is wrong—in the body politic, in ourselves, or in the speakers."*

Hate Speech on the Internet Should Not Be Restricted

by Charles Levendosky

About the author: *Charles Levendosky is the editorial page editor and a syndicated columnist for the* Casper Star-Tribune *in Wyoming.*

Another free speech battle has begun to shape up. This one isn't about sex; it's about hate speech. It pits those who want to prohibit hatemongering on the Internet against those who believe that the First Amendment must protect even that speech—no matter how despicable.

Hate speech on the Internet has grown rapidly—through websites, email, bulletin boards and chat rooms—according to a study published by the Anti-Defamation League last year. The ADL monitors the Internet looking for anti-Semitic speech propagated by neo-Nazi, white supremacist groups. In the study, "High-Tech Hate: Extremist Use of the Internet," the ADL notes that hate websites more than doubled in one year, from 1996 to 1997. The organization estimates their number to be 250. And pressure is mounting to shut down these sites, or at least, to limit access to them.

Curtailing Hate Speech on the Internet

According to a *Washington Post* story dated October 24, 1997, the ADL is working with America Online to develop software to filter out hate sites.

In 1997, the United Nations held a seminar in Geneva to discuss how to curtail hate speech on the Internet.

In April 1998, the Australia B'nai B'rith Anti-Defamation Commission petitioned Australia's Internet Industry Association to make racist websites illegal in that nation.

And on August 2, 1998, the *New York Times* reported that Canada, using that country's anti-hate legislation, has begun cracking down on hate speech on the Internet.

Hate speech can be loosely defined as speech that reviles or ridicules a person

Reprinted with permission from "Bigoted Speech, the Speech We Hate to Defend," by Charles Levendosky, *Gauntlet,* vol. 2, 1998.

or group of people based upon their race, creed, sexual orientation, religion, handicap, economic condition or national origin.

HateWatch also monitors hate-group activities on the Internet. David Goldman, director of HateWatch, estimates that more than 200 active racist, anti-Semitic, anti-gay, Holocaust denial, Christian Identity, black racist, anti-Arab, anti-Christian pages can currently be found on the Internet.

Goldman credits Don Black, the ex-Grand Dragon of the Knights of the Ku Klux Klan's Realm of Alabama with creating the first racist website, Stormfront, in March 1995. Stormfront is still online.

HateWatch has taken a different approach to hate websites. The organization is in the process of "adopting" domain names (URLs) which might otherwise be used by hate groups. They are asking donations to acquire such domain names as "aryan-nations.org," "whitepower.net," and "kukluxklan.net." It's a creative strategy, but one which seems doomed to failure.

> *"One man's hate speech is another man's political statement."*

The range of possible domain names connected to any hate group is only limited by the imagination. If the domain name "whitepower.net" if already registered, one could shift to "snowpower.net," or use "pure-nations.org" for the aryan domain.

At present, the World Wide Web contains skinhead and white supremacist sites with names like Hammerskin Nation, Delaware Skingirl Crew, Orgullo Skinheads, Bootgirl88, Skinhead Pride, SS Bootboys, White Aryan Resistance, White World of Skinchick, Siegheil88, Hatemongers' Hangout, Skinz, Northern HammerSkins. The list tops 130—of just these groups.

There are anti-gay websites with names like The American Guardian, Cyber Nationalist Group (CNG), God Hates Fags, RevWhites Christian Politics, and Society To Remove All Immoral Godless Homosexual Trash (STRAIGHT).

The Internet parade of hate includes the anti-Muslim websites (The Glistrup Homepage and Faelleslisten), the anti-Arab sites (Jewish Defense League and the Kahane Homepage), the anti-Christian sites (Altar of Unholy Blasphemy and Chorazaim), anti-Semitic sites (Radio Islam and Jew Watch), black racist sites (House of David, and The Blackmind), Holocaust denial sites (Adelaide Institute and Annwn Publications), neo-Nazi sites (Alpha and Fourth Reich), and Christian Identity sites (America's Promise Ministries and IaHUeH's Kingdom).

Internet Filters

A number of universities in the United States, more sensitive to people's feelings than the significance of the First Amendment, have written speech regulations to punish students who post hate messages on the World Wide Web. Some universities have put blocking technology on their computers that have Internet access—to filter out websites that advocate racism, anti-Semitism, white supremacy, homophobia, Holocaust denial, sexual superiority, anti-government vigilante justice, and other forms of prejudice and bigotry.

There are those organizations, like the ADL, that push for a rating system for every web page, with stiff fines for those who don't rate their sites or rate them wrongly. Presumably an Aryan Nations or Ku Klux Klan site would have to rate itself (or be rated by others) so that children could not gain access when the appropriate filtering program is installed to read the ratings and block some categories.

The Southern Poverty Law Center in Montgomery, Alabama, recently labelled the Nation of Islam as a hate group in an intelligence report, because of anti-Semitic comments made by Minister Louis Farrakhan.

Interestingly enough, neither the ADL nor HateWatch nor even the Southern Poverty Law Center lists the Jewish Defense Organization as a group that spews hate on its website.

Who makes the decision about which websites cross the line into hate speech? The federal government? Internet service providers?

A few months ago, Microsystems Software, the manufacturer that makes the filter called Cyber Patrol, decided to block out the American Family Association's website because it contains prejudicial statements against homosexuals. The rightwing American Family Association, ironically, has pushed parents, schools and libraries to use Internet filters, including Cyber Patrol.

> *"If hate speech were prohibited, socio-political movements could be crushed before they even started."*

Richard Delgado, Jean Stefancic and other academics argue in *Must We Defend Nazis? Hate Speech, Pornography, and the New First Amendment* that hate speech should not be protected by the First Amendment. Fortunately, their arguments have not been persuasive against our long and honored tradition of free speech.

While we may despise the comments made on some of these hate-filled websites, it is difficult to argue they are not espousing political positions. Often one man's hate speech is another man's political statement. And political commentary has—and should continue to have—the highest First Amendment protection.

White supremacist David Duke, who was recently elected to lead the Republican Party in the largest GOP parish in the state of Louisiana, has a website that denigrates blacks. His political stature is built on his racism. Certainly, his web page, hate and all, is a political statement.

Duke explains why the KKK and other white power groups have flocked to the Internet: "As the new millennium approaches, one can feel the currents of history moving swiftly around us. The same race that created the brilliant technology of the Internet, will—through this powerful tool—be awakened from its long sleep." And, indeed, white supremacist websites are some of the most technologically sophisticated on the Internet.

As the U.S. Supreme Court noted in finding the Communications Decency Act unconstitutional last year, anyone with access to the Internet can be a pamphleteer sending email messages to thousands of recipients with one click of a button, or posting websites that are eventually seen by hundreds of thousands. It is the most democratic communication media yet devised. However, to remain truly democratic, it must allow any viewpoint to be posted and debated.

Outrageous Rhetoric

The leading edge of any social or political movement cuts a path to recognition by using radical, sometimes outrageous rhetoric. The rhetoric is there to define or redefine the landscape in terms that suit that particular movement. It is there to shake up the prevailing state of affairs. This has been true in this nation from the time of our own revolution to gain independence from Great Britain to the present. Certainly, the British Crown could have considered the Declaration of Independence a form of hate speech.

The Industrial Workers of the World, the labor movement, the socialist movement, anti-war movements, the Black Power movement, poverty marches, veteran's marches, the temperance crusade, the women's liberation movement, the anti-abortion movement—all used inflammatory rhetoric like a blowtorch to burn a hole in the status quo. To demand that people take sides. And see the world differently.

If hate speech were prohibited, socio-political movements could be crushed before they even started.

The current cliche about "civility" in debate may be fine when we all agree to basic premises and we're all well-fed and treated equally. We can afford to be polite to one another and even friendly. But civility does not serve the downtrodden, the forgotten, the invisible, the persecuted, the hungry and homeless. Civility in pursuit of justice plays to the power structure's selective deafness. To be effective, the voice must be raised, the tone sharpened, the language at a pitch that slices the air. Americans know this at heart—we were born in a revolution.

Suppressing Speech May Lead to Violence

Hate speech is not the cause of bigotry, but arises out of it and a sense of political and social powerlessness. Allowing those who see themselves as powerless to speak—no matter how vehement the language—salves the speaker. Venting frustration, anger, and hurt is an important use of language. It may actually short circuit an inclination for physical violence.

The black playwright Imamu Amiri Baraka (LeRoi Jones) illustrated this principle in *Dutchman*, a 1960s play about a black rebellion. One of his characters yells at a white woman riding on the same train, "And I'm the great would-

90

be poet. Yes. That's right! Poet. Some kind of bastard literature . . . all it needs is a simple knife thrust. Just let me bleed you, you loud whore, and one poem vanished. . . . If Bessie Smith had killed some white people she wouldn't have needed that music."

Suppressing speech, even hateful speech and perhaps especially hateful speech, would inevitably lead to violence.

We don't protect the civil rights of those who are targets of hateful speech by suppressing the speech of hate mongers. For eventually, inexorably, such suppression turns and bites those it is supposed to protect.

When civil liberties are lost, civil rights follow. When a chunk is carved out of First Amendment protections, we all lose a portion of our rights as citizens.

Speech laws that have been adopted to protect racial minorities are actually used to persecute the very people they were created to protect. This has been true in Great Britain and in Canada—just as it has been true at universities in the United States.

> *"If the federal government were to be given the authority to limit speech on the Internet, that authority would spread to all media."*

When the Supreme Court of Canada adopted the Catharine MacKinnon/ Andrea Dworkin thesis that pornography is harmful to women, the very first groups to be targeted by the Canadian government were gay and lesbian bookstores. Two of Andrea Dworkin's own books (*Woman Hating* and *Pornography: Men Possessing Women*) were seized at the Canadian border by customs officials. The books were adjudged to be "pornography" and thereby harmful to women.

Those who censor others, eventually censor themselves. They bury their own messages.

When the University of Michigan put its speech code against racist speech into effect and before the code was struck down in 1989 as unconstitutional, 20 students were charged with violations. Ironically only one was punished, a black student for using the term "white trash."

It was no accident that the first person to be charged under a U.S. hate crime enhancement law was a black man. It added years to his sentence.

The power structure interprets and enforces the law. Where white males dominate, white males are less likely to be prosecuted under such laws—a cynical observation, but true.

A Dangerous Power

If the federal government were to be given the authority to limit speech on the Internet, that authority would spread to all media. And the government would have the unholy power to stifle dissent and protest.

Suppressing hate speech is more dangerous than allowing it to exist. Like it or not, hate speech has a role to play in a nation dedicated to vigorous debate about public issues.

If we come to a point in our history when we fear messages that we despise, then we will have lost the strength and will to govern ourselves. Or as the great First Amendment scholar Alexander Meiklejohn put it so succinctly when testifying before Congress in 1955, "To be afraid of any idea is to be unfit for self-government."

Chapter 3

Are Federal Hate Crime Laws Necessary?

Overview: Hate Crime Legislation

by Kenneth Jost

About the author: *Kenneth Jost is a staff writer for* CQ Researcher, *a weekly news and research report published by Congressional Quarterly, Inc.*

St. Paul, Minnesota, enacted a local hate crime ordinance in 1982. Instead of adopting the Anti-Defamation League's (ADL) penalty-enhancement model [which provided increased penalties for crimes in which the victim was selected because of race, religion, or sexual orientation], however, St. Paul decided to create a new offense: bias-motivated disorderly conduct. Under the ordinance, anyone who "places on public or private property a symbol, object, appellation, characterization or graffiti" that "arouses anger, alarm or resentment in others on the basis of race, color, creed or religion" was guilty of the misdemeanor offense of disorderly conduct. The city amended the law in 1989 to specifically include a burning cross or a Nazi swastika in the prohibitions and in 1990 to prohibit actions based on sexual prejudice.

Hate Crime or Free Speech

In the summer of 1990, prosecutors invoked the St. Paul ordinance for the first time. A group of teenagers was charged with placing a burning cross in the front yard of Russ and Laura Jones, who had recently become the first black family to move into a white working-class block in East St. Paul. Besides the St. Paul ordinance, the defendants were also charged with committing a racially motivated assault in violation of the state's hate crime law.

The defendants in the case included Robert A. Viktora, then seventeen, a high school dropout and a "skinhead"—a rapidly growing, youth-oriented group that preaches violence against blacks, Jews and gays. Viktora's court-appointed attorney, Edward J. Cleary, decided to challenge the St. Paul ordinance on constitutional grounds. Cleary did not contest the state charge against his client, but he said the local ordinance was overbroad because it directly punished "expressive" conduct. "In a country that values free speech, we should not have a law that says that expressing certain ideas, however offensive they may be, is in itself a crime," Cleary told one reporter.

The Ramsey County [Minnesota] juvenile court judge who heard Viktora's plea agreed and struck the law down. But in January 1991, the Minnesota Supreme Court revived the law. The court narrowly construed the law to apply only to what the U.S. Supreme Court had called in a 1942 case (*Chaplinsky v. New Hampshire*) "fighting words"—words that have "a direct tendency to cause acts of violence by the person to whom, individually, the remark is addressed." Under that construction, the state court concluded, the law was valid.

On June 10, 1991, the U.S. Supreme Court decided to review Viktora's case, which was formally called *R.A.V. v. St. Paul*, since juveniles are ordinarily not identified by name in juvenile court cases. The high court's action signaled a likely inclination to overturn the law. And even many supporters of the law conceded it had problems. The Anti-Defamation League filed a brief defending the law—as narrowed by the Minnesota court—even

> *"The justices voted unanimously to strike down the St. Paul ordinance, but they divided into two camps in explaining the decision."*

though officials acknowledged the ordinance went beyond the ADL's recommended statute.

Ramsey County prosecutor Tom Foley, who was to argue the case before the Supreme Court, also acknowledged the law could not be applied literally. "If the cross had been burned down at the corner, at the middle of the day, at a protest, that's probably not something you could prosecute," Foley told a reporter on the eve of the arguments. "What if it's midnight, and right in front of the Joneses' house? That's closer to the line."

A Divided Court

The Supreme Court's decision on June 22, 1992, however, went further than the parties to the case or most observers had expected. The justices voted unanimously to strike down the St. Paul ordinance, but they divided into two camps in explaining the decision. A minority of four justices concluded that the law was overbroad because, even under the Minnesota court's ruling, it could be applied to protected forms of expression. On that basis, the four justices said, the law had to be struck down, but a narrower one might survive.

A five-justice majority, however, concluded that the ordinance was unconstitutional because it impermissibly singled out for prosecution specific types of expression—racial, religious or sexual insults—on the basis of their content. "The First Amendment does not permit St. Paul to impose special prohibitions on those speakers who express views on disfavored subjects," Justice Antonin Scalia wrote for the majority.

Scalia emphasized that the cross-burning could have been punished under several other laws—some of them carrying stiffer penalties than the St. Paul ordinance. But to pass constitutional muster, he said, any law limiting forms of expression had to be free of "content discrimination." A law targeting a particular kind of bigotry would not pass that test.

The four justices in the minority sharply challenged Scalia's reasoning and indirectly accused him of harboring a broader, unstated agenda. Justice Byron R. White said Scalia's rationale would prevent the use of civil rights laws in cases where racial epithets or sexual harassment created a "hostile work environment." Justice Harry A. Blackmun implied that Scalia's real goal was to nullify campus speech codes. "I fear that the Court has been distracted from its proper mission by the temptation to decide the issue over 'politically correct speech' and 'cultural diversity,' neither of which is presented here," Blackmun wrote.

Some observers outside the court also saw evidence of a conservative agenda in Scalia's opinion—and in the way the justices divided. Scalia led a predominantly conservative bloc that also included Chief Justice William H. Rehnquist and Justices Anthony M. Kennedy, David H. Souter and Clarence Thomas. There was a more liberal cast to the four-justice minority of White, Blackmun, John Paul Stevens and Sandra Day O'Connor.

Supporters of hate crime laws tried to counter a broad reading of the court's decision. ADL officials issued statements saying that hate crimes were still against the law and that their approach of increasing penalties for bias-motivated offenses would be upheld. But before the summer ended, state supreme courts in Wisconsin and Ohio had reached the opposite conclusion and decided to strike down hate crime laws directly modeled after the ADL proposal.

Hate Crime Laws Are Necessary

by Eric Holder

About the author: *Eric Holder is the assistant attorney general of the United States.*

Editor's Note: The following viewpoint is the statement of assistant attorney general Eric Holder before the House Judiciary Committee on Hate Crimes on August 4, 1999. The committee was hearing testimony concerning the passage of H.R. 1082, the Hate Crimes Prevention Act of 1999.

In 1990 and 1994, the committee [House Judiciary Committee] strongly supported the enactment of the Hate Crime Statistics Act and the Hate Crimes Sentencing Enhancement Act. In 1996, the committee responded in time of great national need by quickly enacting the Church Arson Prevention Act.

And I hope that you will respond once again to the call for a stronger federal stand against hate crimes, and that you will join law enforcement officials and community leaders across the country in support of H.R. 1082, the Hate Crimes Prevention Act of 1999.

The Need for Federal Hate Crimes Laws

Now unfortunately, recent events have only reinforced the need for federal hate crimes legislation. We were all horrified at the brutal murders of Billy Jack Gaither in Alabama [in February 1999], Matthew Shepard in Wyoming [in October 1998] and James Byrd in Jasper, Texas [in June 1998].

Just in the weeks since I testified on these issues before the Senate Judiciary Committee in May [1999], a young man linked with a white supremacy organization shot several people in Illinois and Indiana [in July 1999], including a group of Jewish men walking home from sabbath services in Chicago. Two others died from their injuries: Won-Joon Yoon, a student at Indiana University from South Korea, and Ricky Byrdsong, an African-American male who was

Excerpted from testimony given by Eric Holder before the House Judiciary Committee on Hate Crimes, August 4, 1999, in Washington, D.C.

only walking with his daughters near his home in Skokie, Illinois.

In California, three synagogues in Sacramento erupted in flames on the same morning, and Winfield Scott Mowder and Gary Matson, a gay couple, were brutally murdered in the Redding home.

These crimes, and others around the country, are not just a law enforcement problem. They are a problem for our schools, our religious institutions, our civic organizations and also for our national leaders.

When we pool our expertise, experiences and resources together, we can help build communities that are safer, stronger and more tolerant.

Confronting Hate Crimes

First, we must gain a better understanding of the problem. In 1997, the last year for which we have complete statistics, 11,200 law enforcement agencies participated in the data-collection program and reported just over 8,000 hate crime incidents. Eight thousand hate crime incidents are about one hate crime incident per hour.

But we know that even this disturbing number significantly underestimates the true level of hate crimes. Many victims do not report these crimes, and police departments do not always recognize, appropriately categorize or adequately report hate crimes.

Second, we must learn to teach tolerance in our communities so that we can prevent hate crimes by addressing bias before it manifests itself in violent criminal activity. We must foster understanding and should in-

> *"[Hate] crimes . . . are not just a law enforcement problem. They are a problem for our schools, our religious institutions, our civic organizations and also for our national leaders."*

still in our children the respect for each other's differences and the ability to resolve conflicts without violence.

The Department of Education, with the national association of attorneys general, published a guide to confronting and stopping hate and bias in our schools. And I'm also pleased that the department is assisting a new partnership in its efforts to develop a program for middle school students on tolerance and diversity.

Third, we must work together to effectively prevent and prosecute hate crimes.

Now the centerpiece of the administration's hate crimes initiative is the formation of local working groups in the United States attorneys districts around the country. These task forces are hard at work bringing together the FBI, the U.S. Attorney's Office, the Community Relations Service, local law enforcement, community leaders and educators to assess the problem in their area and to coordinate our response to hate crimes.

These cooperative efforts are reinforced by the July 1998 memorandum of understanding between the national district attorney's association and the Department of Justice. Where the federal government does have jurisdiction, the MOU calls for early communication among local, state and federal prosecutors to devise investigative strategies.

Finally, we should never forget that law enforcement has an indispensable role to play in eradicating hate crimes. We must ensure that potential hate crimes are investigated thoroughly, prosecuted swiftly and punished soundly. In order to do this effectively, we must address the gaps that exist in the current federal law.

Two Deficiencies

The principal Federal Hate Crimes Statute, 18 USC Section 245, prohibits certain hate crimes committed on the basis of race, color, religion or national origin. This law has two serious deficiencies.

First, even in the most blatant cases of racial, ethnic or religious violence, no federal jurisdiction exists unless the violence was committed because the victim engaged in one of six federally protected activities. This unnecessary, extra intent requirement has led to acquittals in several cases. It has also limited our ability to work with state and local officials to investigate and prosecute many incidents of brutal, hate-motivated violence.

Any federal legislative response to hate crimes must close this gap.

[The Hate Crimes Prevention Act] would amend Section 245 so that in cases involving racial, religious or ethnic violence, the federal government would have the jurisdiction to investigate and prosecute cases involving the intentional infliction of bodily injury without regard for the victim's participation in one of the six enumerated federally protected activities.

And as I said, this is an essential fix. . . .

Jurisdictional Limitations

We can offer [assistance] to these localities, but in most circumstances, only if we have jurisdiction in the first instance. The level of collaboration achieved between federal and local officials in Jasper, with regard to the James Byrd case, was possible only because we had a [valid] claim of federal jurisdiction in that matter. The state and federal partnership in this case led to the prompt inditcment of three men on state capital charges.

> "*A significant number of hate crimes based on the sexual orientation of the victim are committed every year in this country.*"

The second jurisdictional limitation on Section 245 is that it provides no coverage whatsoever for violent hate crimes committed because of bias based on the victim's sexual orientation, gender or disability, and these crimes pose a serious problem for our nation.

A meaningful federal response to hate crimes must provide protection for these groups and [the Hate Crimes Prevention Act] would do just that. The bill would prohibit the intentional infliction of bodily injury based on the victim's sexual orientation, gender or disability whenever the incident involved or affected interstate commerce.

Not Covered

And we know that a significant number of hate crimes based on the sexual orientation of the victim are committed every year in this country. And despite this fact, 18 U.S.C. 245 does not provide coverage for these victims unless there is independent basis for federal jurisdiction.

We also know that a significant number of women are exposed to brutality and even death because of their gender. The Congress, with the enactment of the Violence Against Women Act in 1994, has recognized that some violent assaults committed against women are bias crimes rather than mere random attacks.

"In those rare instances where states cannot or will not take action, the federal government can step in to assure that justice is done."

And we also know that because of their concern about the problem of disability-related hate crimes, Congress amended the Hate Crime Statistics Act in 1994 to require the FBI to collect information about such hate-based incidents from state and local law enforcement agencies.

Similarly, the federal sentencing guidelines include an upward adjustment for crimes where the victim was selected because of his or her sexual orientation, gender or disability.

[The Hate Crimes Prevention Act] is consistent with recent court decision on Congress' legislative power under Section 5 of the 14th Amendment and is mindful of commerce clause limitations.

The Law Is Constitutional

Congress has the constitutional authority to regulate violent acts motivated by racial or ethnic bias. The bill is also mindful of the traditional role that states have played in prosecuting crime.

Indeed, state and local officials investigate and prosecute the vast majority of the hate crimes that occur in their communities and would continue to do so if this bill was enacted.

But we need to make sure that federal jurisdiction covers everything that it should, so that in those rare instances where states cannot or will not take action, the federal government can step in to assure that justice is done.

It is by working in collaboration that state and federal law enforcement officials stand the best chance of bringing the perpetrators of hate crimes swiftly to justice.

Chapter 3

The Hate Crimes Prevention Act will bring together state, local and federal teams to investigate and prosecute incidents of hate crime wherever they occur.

The enactment of [the Hate Crimes Prevention Act] is a reasonable measure and a necessary response to the wave of hate-based incidents taking place around our country because of biases built on the race, color, national origin, religion, sexual orientation, gender or disability of the victim.

Hate Crime Laws Do Not Threaten Free Speech

by Howard P. Berkowitz

About the author: *Howard P. Berkowitz is national chairman of the Anti-Defamation League, an organization dedicated to preventing racial and ethnic prejudice.*

Hate crimes, whether directed against one person or many, are particularly destructive in the way they spread feelings of hurt, anxiety and fear. A hate crime is more than an attack on an individual. It is an assault on an entire community. And for this reason alone it is important to send a message that criminals who commit bias crimes will pay the price.

Critics of hate-crimes legislation have used colorful prose to dismiss the laws as "identity politics" and "theatrical empathy," arguing the statutes are a strong-handed attempt to impose a politically correct ideology and an affront to basic constitutional rights.

A Serious Problem

However, there has been no shortage of horrifying assaults on blacks, Jews and other minorities, which would seem to call this oversimplified view into question. Crimes predicated on race and ethnicity are becoming more and more virulent in this country. They are being committed by individuals with links to organized hate groups operating on the farthest fringes of American society—groups whose outreach is widening due to advances in technology, most notably the Internet.

The crimes have been shocking in their brutality. A man who, according to police, was bent on issuing a "wake-up call to America to kill Jews" builds up an arsenal capable of wreaking vast amounts of bloodshed and barges—guns blazing—into a Jewish community center. Before his bloody rampage in August 1999 was over, Buford O. Furrow Jr. had shot and wounded 5- and 6-year-olds, a teen-ager and a woman before taking the life of a Filipino-American postal worker whom Furrow identified as a "target of opportunity" because of his race.

Chapter 3

Weeks earlier, Benjamin Nathaniel Smith, an avowed racist with ties to the virulently anti-Semitic and racist World Church of the Creator, had gone on a killing rampage through the Midwest. The targets again were minorities—Orthodox Jews on their way home from synagogue, blacks and Asian-Americans. The carnage resulted in the deaths of former basketball coach Ricky Byrdsong and a Korean-American graduate student, slain as he emerged from church in Bloomington, Indiana.

Smith's targets also were chosen carefully and, like the three synagogues in Sacramento, California, which were damaged by arson in July 1999, his crimes affected people engaged in, or on their way to, worship. Near one of the synagogues in Sacramento, police found hate literature and later discovered evidence possibly linking two brothers arrested in connection with another hate crime—the brutal slaying of a homosexual couple—to the synagogue fires.

All of this hate activity has left us, as Americans, grappling for answers. Everyone agrees that something, legislative or otherwise, must be done to stem the tide of hate. The Anti-Defamation League, or ADL, as a leader in the fight against anti-Semitism, hatred and bigotry, believes strong hate-crimes legislation is one answer. We do not view penalty enhancement as a panacea, a cure-all for the scourge of hate in society. But it is important—a rational, fair-minded message to bigots and racists everywhere—that society will not tolerate crimes that single out an individual because of his or her race, religion, national origin or color. Penalty-enhancement statutes put criminals on notice that the consequences for committing hate crimes are severe.

Aside from sensational crimes, government statistics also make a compelling argument for the necessity of strong hate-crimes statutes. Since 1991 the FBI has documented more than 50,000 hate crimes. In 1996 alone, 8,759 hate crimes were reported in the United States. In 1997, the most recent year for which statistics are available, the number rose to 9,861—the highest number of hate crimes ever recorded by the FBI in a single year. Still many more hate crimes go undocumented. The numbers continue to rise as the casualties mount.

> *"Hate-crimes legislation is important because it is a message from society and the legislature that bias crimes will not be tolerated."*

Legislators across the country, state and federal, recognize the special trauma hate crimes cause, the sense of vulnerability and fear they foster and the polarizing effect they can have on entire communities. Lawmakers understand their responsibility to provide criminal sanctions that reflect our collective societal judgment regarding the relative seriousness of criminal offenses.

While all crimes are upsetting, a hate crime is particularly disturbing because of the unique impact not only on the victim but also on the victim's community. Bias crimes are designed to intimidate, leaving people feeling isolated, vulnerable and unprotected. Failure to address this unique type of crime can cause an isolated incident to explode into widespread community tension. The damage cannot be measured solely in terms of physical injury or dollars and cents. By making minority communities fearful, angry and suspicious of other groups—and of the legal structure that is supposed to protect them—these incidents can damage the fabric of our society and fragment communities.

> *"[Hate-crimes laws] only punish acts of violence; they neither condemn private beliefs nor chill constitutionally protected speech."*

Opponents of hate-crimes legislation often will argue that the laws represent the worst aspects of Orwellian thought control and intrude on the sanctity of the First Amendment. These critics erroneously contend that such statutes punish individuals for their beliefs and their speech. In making this flawed argument, the critics demonstrate a fundamental misunderstanding of hate-crimes legislation as well as the First Amendment.

Speech Is Not a Target

The fact is hate-crimes legislation does not in any way target or punish speech; such statutes punish conduct only. Individuals remain free to express any view about race, religion, sexuality or any other topic. It is only when they act on their prejudices or callously select their victims based on personal characteristics such as race or religion that hate-crimes statutes come into play. Such legislation simply says that someone who attacks a black or a Jew because he is black or Jewish will receive an enhanced penalty. Such an approach by no means is new to criminal law. Legislators, law-enforcement officials and judicial officers frequently consider motive—in charges ranging from the mundane, such as burglary, to the exceptional, such as treason—to determine whether a crime, or what class of crime, has been committed.

The U.S. Supreme Court has supported that view. In 1993, in a landmark 9-0 decision, the court upheld a Wisconsin penalty-enhancement statute, ruling that the state was right in seeking to increase the sentence for an African-American man who had encouraged and participated in an attack on a young white man. In *Wisconsin vs. Mitchell,* the high court ruled that the statute aimed to discourage conduct that is not protected by the First Amendment and that the state had a special interest in punishing bias crimes. The court's decision removed any doubt that legislatures properly may increase the penalties for criminal activity in which the victim is targeted because of his race, religion, sexual orientation, gender, ethnicity or disability.

Important Legislation

Hate-crimes legislation is important because it is a message from society and the legislature that bias crimes will not be tolerated. To date, 40 states and the

District of Columbia have enacted hate-crimes statutes, as has the federal government. The most effective kind of hate-crimes law, often based on model legislation introduced by the ADL, provides for enhanced penalties when a perpetrator chooses his victim based on race, religion or another protected category. When prejudice prompts an individual to engage in criminal conduct, a prosecutor may seek a more severe sentence but must prove, beyond a reasonable doubt, that the victim intentionally was selected because of personal characteristics. The intent of penalty-enhancement hate-crimes laws is not only to reassure targeted groups by imposing serious punishment on hate-crime perpetrators but also to deter these crimes by demonstrating that they will be dealt with seriously and swiftly.

Constitutional and effective penalty-enhancement statutes must continue to be enacted at the federal and state levels. According to the current federal law—18 U.S.C. Sec. 245—before the federal government can prosecute a hate crime, it must prove both that the crime occurred because of a person's membership in a designated group and because (not simply while) the victim was engaged in certain specified federally protected activities, such as serving on a jury, voting or attending public schools. Thus, while federal law protects Americans from hate crimes in voting booths and schools, it does not protect them from similar crimes in their homes or on the streets. Presently, it is left to the discretion of the local officials whether to prosecute the crime as a hate crime.

The Hate Crimes Prevention Act, which the Senate has approved and the president has vowed to sign into law if passed by the House, would make it easier for the federal government to combat hatred. The act would expand the list of protected categories—currently only race, color, religion and national origin—to include real or perceived sexual orientation, gender and disability. Clearly, then, this would empower the federal government to more effectively protect Americans from bias crimes and to step in when local law-enforcement agencies either cannot or will not act to stop hate.

In these increasingly violent times, hate-crimes legislation is a strong and necessary response to combat criminal acts of prejudice and bias. Current hate-crimes laws are both valuable and constitutional. They only punish acts of violence; they neither condemn private beliefs nor chill constitutionally protected speech. The statutes guarantee that perpetrators of bias crimes will be punished in proportion to the seriousness of the crimes they have committed. The laws protect all Americans, allowing them to walk the streets safe in the knowledge that their community will not tolerate violent bigotry.

Hate Crime Laws
May Teach Tolerance

by Patrick Jordan

About the author: *Patrick Jordan is a writer for* Commonweal.

The brutal murder in October 1998 of Matthew Shepard—the twenty-one-year-old gay college student in Wyoming who was beaten and tied to a cross-like fence to die—struck at the conscience of the nation. It was not only the sheer sadism and rancor of the crime that affected Americans, but the sense that Shepard's rights had been violated simply for being who he was.

Crimes and Prejudice

Hate-motivated crimes have their own pedigree, their own smell. They are acts of criminal violence—among them kidnapping, torture, and murder—but their destructive capacity stems from a motivational intensity that sets them apart. When James Byrd, Jr., a disabled African-American, was dragged to his death in Jasper, Texas, in June 1998, every reflective American knew instinctively that this crime was motivated by a particular loathing born of prejudice.

Crimes of this sort can be triggered by a victim's demeanor, color, status, ethnicity, speech, etc., which become the pretext for unleashing blind fury. For potential victims, the threat of such violence is a constant source of vulnerability, unease, fear, even terror. These violent acts of bigotry demand forceful and consistent redress, for they strike at the heart of the solidarity that binds society together; they undermine the very notion of equality.

Twenty-one states [in 1998] have laws that increase the penalties for hate crimes related to race, religion, color, national origin, and sexual orientation. A further nineteen have laws that cover most of the above, but not sexual orientation, even though the F.B.I. reports that 12 percent of hate crimes in 1996 had to do with sexual orientation, and the Southern Poverty Law Center calculates that bias attacks against gays and lesbians are more than twice as likely as similarly motivated attacks on African-Americans, more than six times as likely as those directed at Jews and Hispanics. Ten states, Wyoming among them, have no such laws, and thoughtful people argue they are not needed. In Wyoming, after all, the death penalty is in force for murder, and criminals should be punished for their deeds, not their beliefs.

Antigay Violence Is on the Rise

But whereas the rate of violent crime in general has been falling nationally, violence against gays, lesbians, and transsexuals has been on the rise. Last year in New York City, for example, violent crime fell 10 percent while antigay violence rose by 14 percent, according to the National Coalition of Antiviolence Programs (NCAVP), a gay advocacy group. When a Wyoming legislator likens homosexuals to gay bulls—worthless except to be sent off to the packing plant—the likelihood of a decline in bias crimes is not improved.

Those who question the legality and wisdom of hate-crime legislation, such as columnist George Will, contend that present statutes are sufficient to prosecute hate-motivated crimes, and that to codify "an ever-more elaborate structure of identity politics" will not only prove costly but will enhance divisiveness. Others argue that such statutes diminish the constitutional protection against double jeopardy for the same crime. Still another caveat is that such legislation might limit individuals' free speech. In fact, Matthew Shepard's father, Dennis Shepard, warned after his son's death that legislators should not rush to pass "all kinds of new hate-crime laws. Be sure," he said, "you're not taking away any rights of others. . . ."

> *"Bias-crime laws are less about punishment than about deterrence. Law sends a powerful and effective message that society will not tolerate certain acts."*

Yet, as Will grants, "law has the expressive function of stigmatizing particular conduct." Bias-crime laws are less about punishment than about deterrence. Law sends a powerful and effective message that society will not tolerate certain acts. Brian Levin of Stockton College's Center on Hate and Extremism notes that a Boston statute cut hate crimes by two-thirds. A further consideration concerns local and state officials who fail to assure citizens' rights. When there is an absence of federal oversight, victims may lack adequate recourse. Proponents of the proposed Hate Crimes Prevention Act of 1998 argue that while many local jurisdictions have attempted to respond to hate-motivated violence, the problem is sufficiently serious and widespread to warrant federal intervention. To shield citizens from the double-jeopardy conundrum, [the act] specifically excluded "duplicate punishment for substantially the same offense."

Reasons to Support Hate Crime Laws

There are other reasons to support federal involvement besides the fact that homosexuals suffer higher rates of violent hate crime than any other group. One is that violence against gays is more often directed at their persons than at their property. Whereas the Anti-Defamation League reports that 55 percent of anti-Jewish incidents are against persons, the NCAVP offers evidence that 95 percent of violence against gays is directed at their persons.

Another reason to support such legislation is the matter of who will protect victims when local enforcement agencies are themselves biased. In 1997, only 24 percent of antigay incidents tracked nationally by the NCAVP were reported to the police (half the percentage-rate for reporting violent crime in general) because gays feared going to the authorities. Of those gays who did try to file, 12 percent stated that the local police refused to register their complaints; and of those who actually managed to file, almost half said they had been treated indifferently or with hostility. Worse, according to the NCAVP, incidents of antigay abuse by the police themselves jumped nationally from 266 in 1996 to 468 last year.

The American Jewish Committee (AJC)—no stranger to combating crimes of hate—has noted that proposed federal legislation would continue to leave responsibility for protecting citizens' rights primarily with state and local agencies; and that federal prosecution in hate-crime cases has been used only sparingly in the past (6 percent of incidents). Yet the cumulative effect of such federal laws, the AJC points out, has enhanced deterrence, particularly in states that lack laws or do not enforce them.

The murder of Matthew Shepard was not the first and will not be the last crime of its kind. But it should shake our indifference and lead to actions that reduce such crimes. While legislation itself will not change all hearts, it might send a powerful message to some hate-twisted minds.

Hate Crime Laws Threaten Equal Protection

by Nat Hentoff

About the author: *Nat Hentoff is a columnist for the* Village Voice *and the* Nation *and is the author of* Free Speech for Me—But Not for Thee: How the
American Left and Right Relentlessly Censor Each Other.

Soon after the October 1998 murder of Matthew Shepard, hundreds of
mourners held a vigil in Washington. Chanting "Now! Now! Now!" they demanded that Congress pass the Schumer-Kennedy hate-crimes legislation.

Also supporting the bill is House Democratic leader Richard Gephardt, who
says the law is surely needed. And on October 19, 1998, Attorney General Janet
Reno met with representatives of more than a dozen gay and lesbian groups and
assured them she would renew her call for passage of hate-crimes legislation.

I have appeared on radio and television to debate various representatives of
the ACLU [American Civil Liberties Union] and gay and lesbian groups about
the value and ramifications of laws mandating *additional* prison terms for
crimes designated as having been committed because of hatred of gays, lesbians, the disabled, blacks, Jews, Catholics, et al.

Same Crime, Different Sentences

I start with a case: A young black man was injured so badly during a robbery that he was hospitalized. The perpetrator, a black man, received a prison
sentence.

In another case, in the same city, a white man was assaulted by a black robber
who yelled racial epithets during the attack. That victim was also hospitalized.
Caught and convicted, this black criminal received a longer prison term than the
black man who beat up the young black man.

The mother of the first victim asked an assistant district attorney why the man
who attacked her son so viciously was sentenced to less prison time than the
criminal who beat the white man.

She was told that the assault against the white man was, under law, a hate

Reprinted with permission from "The Case Against Hate-Crimes Laws," by Nat Hentoff, *Village Voice,*
December 15, 1998.

crime and therefore required additional punishment on top of the penalty for the assault itself.

"So," the mother said, "the harm done to my son counts for less than the harm done to the white man."

In a letter to *Newsday* (November 11, 1998), Michael Gorman, a lawyer and a New York City police lieutenant who supports hate-crimes laws, pointed out:

> An antigay hate-crime assault will get much more attention from the district attorney's office and the police department. . . . The criminal penalty often dictates the amount of effort detectives will put into a case, and hate crimes generally warrant more effort, both for the good of society at large and to protect the target victim and his or her identifiable group.

But if the "target victim" has been assaulted by someone bent *only* on robbery or because of a personal dispute—and if there is no evidence that the crime was fueled by bigotry—*that* criminal will get a lesser sentence because the actual criminal assault is not a "hate crime."

What, then, happens to "equal protection of the laws" as it concerns victims of violence?

If you, any of you, are viciously attacked during a robbery or during a "road rage" assault, should the person who did this to you get less prison time because it was not an official "hate crime"?

Double Jeopardy

Furthermore, if the Schumer-Kennedy Hate Crimes Prevention Act becomes law—and I'm reasonably sure it will be passed by the Congress and then signed by the president—there will be an increase in double jeopardy as initially prohibited by the Fifth Amendment to the Constitution:

"Nor shall any person be subject for the same offense to be twice put in jeopardy of life or limb."

The Schumer-Kennedy bill makes violence committed against anyone because of his or her gender, sexual orientation, or disability a federal crime. (The senators' staffs say that other categories of hate crime are covered by previous federal laws.)

This means—as David Harris, executive director of the American Jewish Committee, said in a letter to the *New York Times*—that there will be

"If the Hate Crimes Prevention Act becomes law . . . there will be an increase in double jeopardy as initially prohibited by the Fifth Amendment to the Constitution."

"the need for prosecution at the federal level if and when the local authorities fail to act or when state penalties are inadequate."

Despite the clear wording of the double-jeopardy clause of the Fifth Amendment, the courts have decided that it is lawful to try a person for the same crime in both the state and federal courts. (That has already happened to the police who beat Rodney King, as well as to Lemrick Nelson, for what he did during the Crown Heights riot.)

But it's worth emphasizing what Supreme Court Justice Hugo Black said, in dissent, in *Bartkus v. Illinois* (1959):

> The court apparently takes the position that a second trial for the same act is somehow less offensive [to the Fifth Amendment] if one of the trials is conducted by the federal government and the other by the state. *Looked at from the standpoint of the individual who is prosecuted, this notion is too subtle for me to grasp.* (Emphasis added.)

My argument against the effects of hate-crimes laws does recognize that the Supreme Court has unanimously declared that such legislation and the accompanying double-jeopardy possibilities are constitutional (*Wisconsin v. Mitchell,* 1993). It was a bizarre decision, but that's it.

Why, then, continue the debate? Because it will be useful, when the Schumer-Kennedy bill becomes law, to know what's in store for the nation once the FBI is empowered to deal with alleged hate crimes under this new federalization of those crimes.

Over-intrusive investigations have already taken place in various state prosecutions, such as Illinois (*People v. Lampkin,* 1983). Alleged perpetrators of these crimes have been probed with regard to their past associations, casual remarks, reading habits, and other presumable indications of bigotry. Some of these random invasions of Fourth Amendment privacy protections go back years.

For documentations of these Joe McCarthy–like abuses, see *Hate Crimes: Criminal Law and Identity Politics* (Oxford University Press) by NYU law professor James Jacobs and researcher Kimberly Potter. And white supremacist Tom Metzger advises callers to his telephone hot line to remain silent while committing a bias attack.

Hate Crime Laws Threaten Free Speech

by Melissa Suarez

About the author: *Melissa Suarez is a research associate for the Pope Center for Higher Education Policy, Research Triangle Park, North Carolina.*

The killing in October 1998 of Matthew Shepard has brought to the forefront of debate the idea that a federal law is needed to protect people against "hate crimes." Proponents want the law to punish individuals who target others because of race, sex, religion, disability, or sexual orientation.

The murder of Matthew Shepard of course is tragic. That it was likely committed with hatred for his sexual orientation is indeed also tragic. A federal law against hate crimes, however, could never be constitutional nor could it protect likely victims of such crimes.

Unconstitutional

The U.S. Supreme Court has already unanimously struck down a hate-crime law. *R.A.V. v. City of St. Paul* involved a city ordinance in St. Paul, Minnesota, that prohibited the display of a symbol that arouses "anger, alarm or resentment in others on the basis of race, color, creed, religion or gender."

Several white youths were charged with violating that ordinance when they burned a cross on the property of a black family. The flaw with the ordinance was that it was neither content-neutral (concerned not with the speech's content, but where, when, or how it takes place) nor viewpoint-neutral. Writing for the Court, Justice Antonin Scalia said the ordinance was invalid because "it prohibits otherwise permitted speech solely on the basis of the subjects the speech addresses."

Content and viewpoint neutrality will derail fixture hate-crime laws as well. The best alternative would be to heed Scalia's words, when he wrote that governments have no authority "to license one side of a debate to fight freestyle, while requiring the other to follow the Marquis of Queensbury Rules."

Reprinted with permission from "Crimes of the Mind," by Melissa Suarez, *Freeman*, March 1999.

Campus Speech Codes

Consider how similar legislation, specifically "hate-speech" codes at colleges and universities, have fared. Campus speech codes that punish students for speech, slurs, or epithets that relate to a person's race, gender, religion, or sexual orientation are prime candidates for lawsuits because they, too, lack content and viewpoint neutrality.

The most famous incident involving hate speech began in January 1993 at the University of Pennsylvania. Five black, female students claimed they were victims of racism after a fellow student, Eden Jacobowitz, who was interrupted in his studying by their boisterous behavior outside his window, yelled at them, "Shut up, you water buffalo." Jacobowitz was charged with violating Penn's speech code, which prohibited racial harassment.

> *"[Hate-speech codes] are usually so vaguely worded that the ban is generally on hate speech only by speakers of a certain gender and certain races."*

The administrative judicial officer in charge of his case, in a telling question, asked him if he was "having racist thoughts" when he used the term "water buffalo," because, the administrator said, a water buffalo is a dark, African animal. Jacobowitz vehemently denied his remarks were racist, saying that the students' noise and not their race prompted his remark. Several scholars rushed to Jacobowitz's defense, including black professors at Penn who said there were no racial connotations behind the term "water buffalo." Others pointed out that the water buffalo is found not in Africa but in Asia.

Nevertheless, because of the code, Jacobowitz's fate depended on the black students' interpretation of his remark. They decided it was racist, so the university charged Jacobowitz with racial harassment. The university eventually dropped the charges.

Another problem that hate-speech codes have, and hate-crime laws inevitably would have, is related to their lack of viewpoint neutrality. These codes are not all-inclusive. They are usually so vaguely worded that the ban is generally on hate speech only by speakers of a certain gender and certain races, sexual orientations, religions, or handicaps.

Sheldon Hackney, who was president of the University of Pennsylvania during the "water buffalo" incident, blatantly admitted the codes' selectivity. When someone asked Hackney if "racial harassment" would include "someone [who] called a black with white friends an 'Uncle Tom' or an 'Oreo,' or if someone called a white person a '[expletive] fascist white male pig?'" Hackney said no.

Punishing Thoughts, Not Acts

A federal hate-crime law would also threaten selective enforcement. Such a law could easily be used to protect only certain groups and punish only certain crimes as hate crimes, thereby making some forms of "hate" more punishable than others.

The alternative would be to punish all hate crimes equally, which would be impossible. It would also be superfluous. For example, in Shepard's case, there are already laws against murder, and the penalties are greater than those of any proposed hate-crime legislation.

Nevertheless, many people argue that a federal law against hate crime could possibly stimulate education about racism, sexism, homophobia, and the like. It would also, they say, probably make minorities feel more protected. It's known in some circles as "thought control."

Consider the success of hate-speech codes in this area. At many institutions, students who violate the speech code are required to take classes on the dangers of prejudice and stereotypes. At UCLA, for example, violators of the university's anti-harassment policy usually must either perform several hours of community service or "become educated" about harassment. One student accused of sexual harassment had to establish a program to educate his fraternity about sexual harassment and write a paper for the dean of students on heterosexism and the origins of programs that combat sexual harassment. Similar punishments are handed down at other universities.

One wonders what kinds of "community service" and "education" violators of a federal hate-crime law would be subjected to. After the federal government charged an individual with having the wrong thoughts (which is already a blatantly unconstitutional action), would it then force him to change his mind? The last government to do that was Ingsoc, in George Orwell's *Nineteen Eighty-Four*.

Supporters of hate-crime laws also argue that federal legislation might heighten awareness about prejudices and stereotypes. More important, they say, stiffer penalties for those who commit such crimes would deter them to begin with. How could they serve as a deterrent when the act itself is already a crime?

> *"After the federal government charged an individual with having the wrong thoughts . . . would it then force him to change his mind?"*

A federal hate-crime law would also raise questions of double jeopardy. If, for instance, a black person's accused assailant is acquitted at the state level, he could be retried for the same crime in federal court under the hate-crime law.

We can never know for certain the motive behind a person's speech or action. For that and other reasons, laws designed to punish the thought behind the crime are dangerous and inappropriate in a free society.

Hate Is Not a Crime

by *First Things*

About the author: First Things *is a monthly journal published by Religion and Public Life, an interreligious research and education institute.*

It is a sad story, and what they did to him was despicable. These guys were drinking in a Laramie bar and University of Wyoming freshman Matthew Shepard reportedly made a pass at one of them, whereupon two young men took him out, brutally beat him, robbed him, and left him tied to a fence. A few days later, he died in hospital. It immediately became a nationwide cause celebre for gay and lesbian groups agitating for hate-crime laws that include "sexual orientation." Mr. Shepard's father expressed the hope that nobody would exploit his son's death in order to push an agenda, but the agitators knew when they had come across a good thing. The lead editorial in our establishment paper was titled "Murdered for Who He Was."

The editors remind us that African-Americans, Asians, Jews, Italians, Irish, and others have been victims of hatred. "Gradually, crimes motivated by hate have come to be seen as a category of their own." It apparently took the editors some time to recognize that few such crimes are motivated by love. As to "Who He Was," the editors describe young Shepard as being "slight, trusting, and uncertain how well he would be accepted as an openly gay freshman." They add that he had spent time in Europe and "spoke three languages or more." The point being made, it seems, is that this is not just another black or Puerto Rican kid who was brutally beaten and killed. The editors are saying that he is one of us. This is a young man with whom we can, as it is said, identify. This is a murder that matters.

The editors continue, "He died in a coma yesterday, in a state without a hate-crimes law." It is hard to know what to make of that. He might have pulled out of it if Wyoming had a hate-crimes law? "Hatred can kill," the editors portentously announce. Noted for the record. Observing with satisfaction that the killers will be tried for first-degree murder, the *Times*, which is otherwise adamantly opposed to the death penalty, adds, "But his death makes clear the need for hate-crime laws to protect those who survive and punish those who at-

Reprinted with permission from "Why Hate Crimes Are Wrong," *First Things,* January 1999.

tack others, whether fatally or not, just because of who they are." Apparently it needs to be made clear that beating people up and killing them is against the law. And, if it is done because of "who they are," maybe the perpetrators should be executed more than once?

Hate Is Not a Crime

The admitted purpose of gay agitation for hate-crime laws is to have homosexual acts (which in the real world define "sexual orientation") put on a par with religion, race, gender, and age as a legally protected category. There are many good reasons for thinking that a bad idea. But the very idea of "hate crimes" is highly dubious. Hate is a sin for which people may go to Hell. It is quite another thing to make it a crime for which people should go to jail. The law rightly takes motivation into account; for instance, whether someone is killed by accident or by deliberate intent. In the latter case, malice of some sort is almost always involved, but it is not the malice that makes the killing a crime. A murderer may have nothing personal against someone whom he kills for his money.

It is generally wrong to disapprove of people because of their religion, race, or gender, but it is not a crime.

> *"Hate is a sin for which people may go to Hell. It is quite another thing to make it a crime for which people should go to jail."*

(An exception may be disapproval of someone whose religion includes committing terrorist acts.) The purpose of the gay movement and its advocates, such as the *Times,* is to criminalize disapproval of homosexual acts, or at least to establish in law that such disapproval is disapproved. Most Americans, it may safely be assumed, disapprove of homosexual acts. It is not within the competence of the state to declare that they are, for that reason, legally suspect. In a sinful world, sundry hatreds, irrational prejudices, and unjust discriminations abound. The homosexual movement is notable for its venting of hatred against millions of Americans whom it accuses of being "homophobic." In whatever form it takes, hatred toward other people must be deplored and condemned. But it is utterly wrongheaded to try to make hatred illegal.

Thinking Twice About Outlawing Hate

David Morrison, writing in the *New York Post,* offers a further reason for thinking more than twice about laws against hate crimes. He notes *Newsweek*'s report that Mr. Shepard seems to have had a history of approaching "straight" men for sex. There is, says Morrison, who describes himself as a "former gay activist," a substantial subculture of the gay subculture that goes in for "rough trade"—cruising in public places for sex with straight or semi-straight toughs. He writes, "Yet the fact that a significant number of men strongly desire and pursue public sex under occasionally dangerous circumstances should influence the ongoing conversation, spurred by Shepard's death, about the necessity or wisdom of including sexual orientation in hate-crimes laws. . . . Americans should think long and hard about making the feeling of repugnance at an unwanted sexual advance subject to additional penalties under the law. There is an old saying that hard cases make bad law. It seems to me that the 1990s have provided a corollary: Tragic cases can make bad laws more quickly. Americans should examine the calls for additional hate-crime legislation with extreme care. There is more at stake than any simple claim of human rights."

Martin Luther King, Jr. used to say, "The law cannot make you love me, but it can prevent you from lynching me. And, if you don't lynch me, you may eventually come to love me." We should certainly love our gay brothers, even as we disapprove of the acts that define them as gay. Loving them includes our saying, always lovingly, that they are wrong in trying to use the law to stigmatize those who disapprove of what they do, which is not, the *Times* to the contrary, the only or the most important thing that determines "who they are."

Chapter 4

Which Groups Pose a Threat to Society?

Chapter Preface

Two brothers, Benjamin Williams and James Williams, are suspects in the June 1999 arson attacks on three synagogues in Sacramento and in the murders of a gay couple in northern California. Benjamin Smith shot and killed himself a few weeks later after a high-speed chase with police who believed that he was responsible for a shooting spree in Indiana and Illinois that wounded seven and killed two, all minorities. In August 1999, Buford O. Furrow admitted to police that he walked into a Jewish community center in Los Angeles and opened fire, wounding four children and the center's receptionist. After fleeing the scene, he is also believed to have shot and killed a Filipino-American mail carrier.

Although these incidents in the summer of 1999 occurred in different parts of the United States, the men involved have one thing in common—they all belonged to white supremacist groups. The Williams brothers and Smith were members of the World Church of the Creator (WCOTC), while Furrow was a member of Aryan Nation (AN). Hate group watchdogs such as the Anti-Defamation League, Southern Poverty Law Center (SPLC), and HateWatch contend that white supremacist groups such as WCOTC, AN, and White Aryan Resistance are directly responsible for attacks on blacks, gays, and other minorities. According to Danny Welch, director of the SPLC's Klanwatch project, which monitors hate groups, "The number one reason why we go after the [World Church of the Creator] is because they instill violence in people through their rhetoric." Furthermore, Klanwatch maintains, much of the hate-based terrorism and violence—including murder—suffered by minorities is a direct result of a conspiracy between WCOTC leaders—who advocate violence—and the group's members who act on their leaders' urgings.

However, law enforcement authorities are struggling to find proof that white supremacist groups are behind the violent attacks on minorities and gays. White supremacist groups such as World Church of the Creator and Identity Christian are very careful to state that although they believe the white race is superior to all others, they do not condone or advocate violence against Jews, gays, and minorities. According to the WCOTC, "It is the program of the Church of the Creator to keep expanding the White Race and keep crowding the mud races [minorities] without necessarily engaging in any open warfare or without necessarily killing anybody. . . . Nowhere . . . do we ever suggest killing anybody."

Whether or not white supremacist and other organizations charged with being hate groups are responsible for the violence committed by their members against gays, blacks, and other minorities are among the issues debated in the following chapter.

Hate Groups Do Not Pose a Serious Threat

by David A. Lehrer

About the author: *David A. Lehrer is regional director of the Anti-Defamation League of B'nai B'rith in Los Angeles.*

The cameras and satellite dishes have barely left the North Valley Jewish Community Center in Granada Hills, California. The confessed culprit, Buford O. Furrow Jr., has turned himself in. Yet conclusions are already being drawn that betray an ignorance of the implications of the tragic incident in August 1999.

Acts of Violent Desperation

The message to be drawn from Furrow's rampage is not that extremists are about to overtake America, or that Jewish and other minority institutions ought to become fortresses, or that hate crimes are on the rise, or that anti-Semitism is increasing. The message is these attacks are acts of violent desperation on the part of those who are not succeeding in swaying the world to their views. What we must never do is allow them to dictate how we run our lives and view the world.

Bigotry and hate can warp a person's perspective to the point that 5-, 6- and 7-year-old children can be seen as enemies to be slaughtered. The prism of religious and racial hate can so distort a person's perspective that young innocents become the incarnation of evil, deserving—indeed, demanding—elimination.

The connection of the alleged assailant to the Aryan Nations and the Silent Brotherhood makes all too much sense. These are hate groups with an ideology that justifies violence against those whom they view as the "seed of the devil" (Jews) and "mud people" (African Americans and other minorities). Their track record of violence and inflammatory rhetoric has been well documented and undoubtedly will be extensively explored in the days ahead.

But in a larger context, the nether world of hate has a very limited and narrowly defined constituency that, in large part, acts out of a perverted and desperate effort to attract media and public attention.

In August 1999, I testified at the "State of Human Relations 2000" hearings of

Reprinted with permission from "Tolerance, Not Hate, Is on the Rise," by David A. Lehrer, *Los Angeles Times,* August 13, 1999.

the [Los Angeles] city Human Relations Commission. At that time, I said that the Anti-Defamation League had been monitoring anti-Semitic hate crimes for more than 20 years, and the number over the past several years has been steadily declining, although there have been occasional up-ticks. Our concerns focus mainly on the increased virulence of the individual acts that are being committed.

The hate incidents of 15 and 20 years ago tended to be swastika daubings, cross-burnings and inflammatory graffiti that outrage and hurt a community. Of late, the hate crimes tend to be more violent, more intense and reflective of more than casual racial or religious animus.

The events [in Granada Hills], as well as in the past months in Sacramento, the Midwest and Redding, are symptomatic of the qualitative change in the nature of hate crimes.

Not a Serious Threat

The context of the Granada Hills rampage argues forcefully for what conclusions ought to be drawn. As our research indicates, members of the Aryan Nations and like groups feel more alienated from society now than ever. Their numbers are stagnant or dwindling. They focus on the extreme fringes who might find their message appealing and on young people who may be too guileless to understand the danger of their facile solutions to complex problems (the World Church of the Creator's Web page has a special section for kids).

Their world is a minutely small, incestuous circle of ideological soul mates who have no compunction about sanctioning violence to make their racist and anti-Semitic points—and who speak mainly to themselves.

They have no potential of being a serious political force or of galvanizing American public opinion (a recent ADL national survey of anti-Semitism found historic low levels of anti-Jewish attitudes). In a society in which tolerance has become a mantra, their message doesn't play well. The threat posed by these groups is one of isolated violence, not of a meaningful political movement.

> *"The threat posed by [hate] groups is one of isolated violence, not of a meaningful political movement."*

We have to redouble our efforts to understand that terror can occur and to take security seriously. But we should not isolate ourselves or build fortresses. And, most important, we must recommit ourselves to educating our children about tolerance, diversity and the dangers of hate so that the potential audience for the bigots, no matter how young, is ever smaller.

Exaggerated fear and predictions of an America overcome by hate are the responses that the Furrows of the world hope to elicit. We must not offer them that victory.

121

Individuals Are Responsible for Most Hate Crimes

by Jo Thomas

About the author: *Jo Thomas is a reporter for the* New York Times.

After the 1995 Oklahoma City bombing, law enforcement officials began struggling with a big unanswered question: Were domestic terrorist attacks by white supremacists, both actual and thwarted, isolated events, or the work of a cohesive underground movement?

Federal and state investigators, including undercover agents, have painstakingly searched the evidence in a growing list of bombings, shootings and robberies. But they maintain that there is no evidence of an organized effort among the disparate assortment of violent right-wing groups and individuals scattered across the country.

Leaderless Resistance

Instead, top-level law enforcement officials and experts on terrorism say, what has emerged is a new style of "leaderless resistance"—long urged by white supremacist leaders—of very small cells, pairs or individuals, called lone wolves, acting independently. Hate groups, often using the Internet, provide the philosophical framework. Individuals with few or no tangible connections to these groups do the killing.

Buford O. Furrow Jr., the angry, unemployed white supremacist who the police say scouted several Jewish institutions before shooting five people in a Los Angeles Jewish community center in August 1999, may be the latest example.

The police are not yet saying whether Mr. Furrow fancied himself a lone wolf, part of something larger, or whether, as some suggest, he was just a deeply disturbed loner susceptible to the influences of the violent right. But the actions he has admitted to have focused attention on what officials say is a new and particularly dangerous tactic of supremacists.

"We've moved into the era of the solo act," said Mike Reynolds, an analyst at the Southern Poverty Law Center, a private nonprofit group based in Montgomery, Alabama, that tracks the activities of hate groups around the country.

The notion being preached in pamphlets, on telephone lines and on white supremacist Web sites is that of the romantic, heroic loner who fights his own private war, committing violent acts against the Government, Jews and racial minorities. A warrior working alone, supremacist leaders say, cannot be betrayed or infiltrated by the Federal Bureau of Investigation, a fate that has befallen some hate groups.

> *"Individuals with few or no tangible connections to [hate] groups do the killing."*

"Good hunting, lone wolves," said a telephone message put out on August 3, 1999, by Tom Metzger, the leader of White Aryan Resistance, or W.A.R., a white supremacist group based in California.

Mr. Metzger was deploring the demise of Proposition 187, a California referendum barring illegal immigrants from receiving government services. A Federal court found much of the proposition unconstitutional, and Gov. Gray Davis agreed to drop an appeal of that ruling. Mr. Metzger, in his phone message, said: "Today, California ceased to exist as an Aryan-dominated state. W.A.R. releases all associates from any constraints, real or imagined, in confronting the problem in any way you see fit." He then called for a second civil war.

Mr. Reynolds, of the law center, was among the first to take note when three white supremacists who had bombed a bank, a newspaper and an abortion clinic in Spokane, Washington, in 1996 called themselves Phineas Priests.

The idea that men who feel they are called by God should commit independent acts of terrorism was put forward by Richard Kelly Hoskins, a former member of the American Nazi Party, in a 1990 book, *Vigilantes of Christendom,* which argues that God forbids any mixing of the races. Mr. Hoskins cited Phineas, who in the Old Testament slew an interreligious couple and was rewarded by God with an everlasting priesthood. Mr. Hoskins broached the idea in an earlier book, *War Cycles/Peace Cycles,* an anti-Semitic treatise found in the van abandoned in Los Angeles by Mr. Furrow.

When Mr. Furrow was arrested, he told the F.B.I. he wanted the shootings at the community center to be "a wakeup call to America to kill Jews," officials said.

The Internet's Influence

Terrorism experts point out that advances in technology, in particular the Internet, have fueled the activities of loners, making it easy for them to communicate and gain access to extremist philosophers.

"It puts them all in the loop," said Rabbi Marvin Hier, dean and founder of the Simon Wiesenthal Center in Los Angeles, which monitors 2,100 hate sites on the Web. "They feel linked up. They're not alone. It makes them part of a greater thing. It's their ticket to the world."

Brian Jenkins, an adviser on issues of crime and terrorism to the president of the Rand Corporation, a nonpartisan research organization, said an important consequence of the new technology was the disappearance of hierarchy.

Mr. Jenkins sees a move away from groups modeled after the military, like the Red Brigades, the ultra-left-wing organization responsible for dozens of terrorist attacks in the 1970's and 80's, including the assassination of former Prime Minister Aldo Moro of Italy.

"We've moved into a realm where we are obliged to speak of universes of like-minded fanatics," Mr. Jenkins said, "from which emerge small galaxies of conspirators, or in some cases, simply individuals who mentally incorporate the belief systems, whether it's racism or anti-Semitism or religious fanaticism, of the broader universe, but are not receiving orders in any formal sense of the term."

The danger has increased, Mr. Jenkins said, "because they are virtually impossible to identify in advance."

The worst terrorist act on American soil, the bombing of the Federal building in Oklahoma City, which killed 168 people, was committed by two people, according to the F.B.I.

> *"The notion being preached . . . is that of the romantic, heroic loner who fights his own private war, committing violent acts against the Government, Jews, and racial minorities."*

Found in the belongings of Terry L. Nichols, convicted in that bombing along with Timothy J. McVeigh, was a well-thumbed copy of *Hunter,* a novel by William Pierce, the head of the neo-Nazi National Alliance, who also wrote *The Turner Diaries,* which prosecutors said was a virtual blueprint for the bombing.

The Solitary Killer

Hunter dramatized the idea of the solitary white warrior and was dedicated to Joseph Paul Franklin, a serial killer who shot interracial couples and also wounded the civil rights leader Vernon E. Jordan Jr. and the publisher of *Hustler* magazine, Larry Flynt. Mr. Franklin, who has admitted to or is suspected in 17 murders, is on death row. His first known attack was the bombing of a synagogue in 1977.

The danger of terrorists operating alone or in pairs became a major concern to law enforcement after the bombing in Oklahoma City, particularly in cases in which the attackers had ready access to weapons or explosives and could operate far outside the mainstream, without jobs, home addresses, telephone numbers or credit cards.

Historically, the F.B.I. and other law enforcement agencies geared to identifying and thwarting criminal organizations, like the Mafia, have had far less ability to investigate political groups or their leaders, whose speeches and writings, while inflammatory, are constitutionally protected.

"There is no way to track these people without a massive invasion of privacy," said Paul Bresson, an F.B.I. spokesman in Washington. He added, "Neither the American public nor the F.B.I. wants that."

Federal guidelines adopted in the aftermath of abuses committed in the civil rights and antiwar era bar the F.B.I. from spying on hate groups or infiltrating them unless they have grounds to suspect a group plans to commit a crime.

Within these guidelines, Federal agencies have used undercover agents to thwart a number of attacks planned since the Oklahoma bombing, offering evidence of just how much easier it is to investigate a group, as opposed to keeping track of individuals.

Arrests have been made in groups of from 3 to 12 members on charges of planning to blow up Government and other buildings. Undercover work stopped a plot to bomb the F.B.I.'s national fingerprint records center in West Virginia and another plan, in 1997, to attack an open house at Fort Hood on the Fourth of July.

Interception Is Difficult

But recent hate crimes and acts of terror, the experts say, demonstrate the difficulty of intercepting a lone terrorist and the devastation that can be wreaked by one or two people.

Benjamin Matthew Williams, 31, and his brother James Tyler Williams, 29, arrested in connection with the July 1999 shotgun killings of a gay couple near Redding, California, are also suspects, the police say, in fires that caused nearly $1 million in damage to three synagogues in Sacramento, California, on June 18, 1999.

Another supremacist, Benjamin Nathaniel Smith, 21, who went on a shooting attack against blacks, Asians and Jews in Illinois and Indiana over the Fourth of July weekend in 1999, killed two people and injured nine before killing himself.

Another loner, Eric Robert Rudolph, a fugitive who disappeared into the Carolina woods, is charged with four bombings that left two people dead,

"Advances in technology, in particular the Internet, have fueled the activities of loners, making it easy for them to communicate and gain access to extremist philosophers."

including a police officer, and 124 injured. These attacks included the bombing at Centennial Olympic Park in Atlanta in 1996, the bombings of an Atlanta abortion clinic and of a nightclub with a gay clientele in 1997, and the bombing of an abortion clinic in Birmingham, Alabama, in 1998.

Extensive files from the Internet about Mr. Rudolph were found among the possessions of David Copeland, an engineer who was charged with three mail-bomb attacks on ethnic minorities and homosexuals in London in April 1999. Three people were killed and more than 100 were injured.

Chip Berlet, the president of Political Research Associates, a company based in Somerville, Massachusetts, that tracks extremist groups, said the approaching millennium has focused "a confluence of demonization, scapegoating and conspiracy theories. For people with an ideology that is apocalyptic, the struggle between good and evil is approaching."

Hate groups in this country, Mr. Berlet said, are grounded in a narrative in which "hardy white male middle-class people are being squeezed by secret elites above who manipulate their lives, while down below are lazy, shiftless parasites that are picking their pockets. They feel squeezed from above and below."

"Recent hate crimes and acts of terror . . . demonstrate the difficulty of intercepting a lone terrorist and the devastation that can be wreaked by one or two people."

Mr. Furrow was for a time associated with the Church of Jesus Christ Christian/Aryan Nations. The group espouses the Christian Identity theology, which teaches that people of color were created before Adam and are, therefore, like beasts of the field, and that Jews are the product of a union between Eve and Satan.

The language of Christian Identity "not only demeans minorities and Jews," said Gail L. Gans, director of the Civil Rights Information Center of the Anti-Defamation League, "it sets them up as targets. When you've erased someone's humanity, it makes them easier to shoot."

Anti-Hate Groups Promote Hate and Violence

by Samuel Francis

About the author: *Samuel Francis is a syndicated columnist.*

Now if it's "extremism" you want, search no further than the Holocaust Memorial Museum in Washington, where last week a gentleman named Mark Potok discoursed on the subject of "hate crimes."

Potok, an articulate and well-informed young man, is the publications director of an outfit known as the Southern Poverty Law Center, which makes it its business to sniff out and expose "hate groups." What was odd about the event is that it was Potok—not necessarily the groups he talked about—who turned out to be the extremist.

Hate and Extremism

Potok is an extremist because it appears to be his conviction—indeed, his unshakable and unquestioned assumption—that virtually everyone who disagrees with the political agenda of the left is part of what he called the "Hate Movement," which is identical to the "White Supremacy Movement." Neither "Hate" nor "White Supremacy" nor several other key terms were ever defined, but I would guess you get the drift of who he was talking about.

Potok did indeed discourse on the obvious instances of "hate" in the United States—the murder in Jasper, Texas, of a black man by a white man for apparently racial reasons and several other atrocities directed mostly at non-whites by whites or at homosexuals by heterosexuals. He paid little attention to whites attacked or murdered by non-whites for the same kind of reasons, but leave that point aside.

The reason Potok is an extremist is that he doesn't limit his census of hate to these clear, if one-sided, examples of it. His concept of hate also includes people who have never committed any violent act at all, who don't advocate violence and whose ideas don't even imply or suggest violence. Two of those whom he tried to implicate in the "Hate Movement" were Pat Robertson and Gary Bauer.

Reprinted from "Hate Is Left's Codeword for 'Conservative,'" by Samuel Francis, *Conservative Chronicle*, March 17, 1999. Copyright ©1999 by Creators Syndicate. Reprinted with permission from author and Creators Syndicate.

Both of these gentlemen—the former the founder of the Christian Coalition, the latter the head of the Family Research Council in Washington, and both of them major players on the "religious right"—devote a lot of energy to resisting abortion and challenging the morality of homosexuality. Neither seems to harbor the least interest in race or race-related questions, and neither has ever advocated violence, illegality, "hate" or anything like them.

But, said Potok, Pat Robertson, by his moral and religious condemnations of homosexuality, "provides the moral atmosphere" for such brutal murders as that of homosexual Matthew Shepard in Wyoming in 1998. And on the very day that Shepard's body was discovered, Potok informed us, Gary Bauer even held a press conference to announce a campaign to encourage practicing homosexuals to convert to heterosexuality. "It all leads to Wyoming," Potok warned ominously.

The Spreading "Hate Movement"

Some years ago, Potok revealed, there was a "secret meeting" of "white supremacists" who agreed that they should do more than just blather about blacks and Jews. Gun control, for instance, was an issue they decided to take up, and Potok claims this is where the militia movement came from. The trend within the "Hate Movement," properly understood, you see, is toward the "interaction of different issues," so that even nonracial, non-hateful causes are really only masks for hatred and murder.

> *"The moral atmosphere [anti-hate groups] are trying to create is one that excludes from discussion anyone and any issue they disagree with."*

It's not just opposition to abortion, homosexuality and gun control that Potok tried to smear. He also dragged in opposition to big government and immigration, as well as anybody who defends the display of the Confederate Flag or other traditional Southern symbols. No matter what such activists say or how many disavowals of racism, hatred and violence they issue, Potok has sniffed them out. They're all part of the "Hate Movement," which is growing bigger and bloodier every year.

It soon became clear that by Potok's way of thinking, anyone who disagrees with the agenda he favors is a hater. Potok talked about the "300 years of oppression" and the United States' "history of apartheid enforced by terror," which more or less tips you off to where he stands politically. His purpose in "exposing hate" also became clear—to drive from national political dialogue and participation anyone who questions or challenges the agenda of the left.

The Real Extremists

And that is why Potok and the Southern Poverty Law Center—not the innocent conservatives they smear as "providing the moral atmosphere" for murder—are the real extremists. The moral atmosphere Potok and the SPLC are trying to create is one that excludes from discussion anyone and any is-sue they disagree with and enforces the cultural hegemony of the left in American politics.

If they get away with it, politics will cease to be real politics and become merely a monologue in which Potok and his friends are the only voice you're allowed to hear.

Religious Conservatives Promote Hate and Violence

by Sarah J. McCarthy

About the author: *Sarah J. McCarthy is a freelance writer.*

Religious conservatives are angry at widespread accusations that their holy wars against gays and abortion doctors have created a climate that encourages violence. "The constant degrading of homosexuals is exacting a toll in blood," says *Newsweek* columnist Jonathan Alter—an assertion that conservative columnist Don Feder denounces as "bizarre." Does Alter actually think, asks Feder, that, if some "yahoo in the hinterlands" believes the religious institutions that declare homosexuality a disorder, he'll have "to go out and bash a queer"? Well, not exactly, Mr. Feder.

Those yahoos in the hinterlands who robbed, killed, and tied Matthew Shepard to a fence post may have been just as influenced by class envy, aimed at rich kids whose parents send them to prestigious schools—as Shepard's did—while the losers in life's lottery collect aluminum cans for a living or fish for catfish in the boondocks. Feder probably doesn't think it's bizarre when someone argues that class-envy rhetoric, aimed at rich people or store owners, has exacted a toll in blood, at times leading to the incitement of armed robberies, burglaries, riots, lootings, rebellions, and even violent revolutions.

The Power of Words

When conditions were right, entire nations have been incited by incendiary speech to exterminate whole categories of their fellow humans—for one reason or another. Every one of these mass-murder movements had intellectual or religious organizations that provided the justification for their brand of "purifying" their nation. Speech, as Feder knows, is a powerful thing. Why else would he write columns?

According to a *Newsweek* poll, six out of ten Americans believe the inflammatory rhetoric of the anti-abortion movement has led to a climate in which abortion clinics are more likely to be targeted for violence. A similar number

Reprinted with permission from "Fertile Ground for Terrorists?" by Sarah J. McCarthy, *Humanist*, January/February 1999.

think the government should be doing more to protect abortion clinics. Pat Buchanan, however, denies that his fellow social conservatives have played any part in fanning the flames. His denial comes as clinics are besieged with a flurry of shootings and bombings, threats of anthrax in the mail, and radical priests like the Reverend Donald Spitz of Pro-Life Virginia pronouncing the sniper who killed abortion provider Dr. Barnett Slepian in Amherst, New York, "a hero."

What if there were a pro-choice website similar to the real anti-abortion website that encourages true believers to kill abortion doctors? One can only begin to imagine the hue and cry that would ensue if Buchanan or Feder were to discover that pro-choice proponents were encouraging the killing of anti-abortionists, with lines through the names of those already killed and the names of the living, their children, and addresses.

Buchanan and other conservatives have written robust articles about the insidious dangers of rap music and Hollywood values that have led to cultural pollutants like promiscuity, drug use, and the rape and degradation of women. During his 1992 presidential campaign, Buchanan commented in a speech that the Los Angeles riots were the work of "a mob that came out of rock concerts where rap music celebrates raw lust and cop killing." How is the rhetoric about killing gays and abortion providers different?

If people were not influenced by words and ideas, there would be no point in having schools, churches, or advertisements. The more respected an institution, the more power of persuasion it holds over the actions of its followers. But to pound away at the idea that one group should be targeted as special sinners deserving of ridicule is not a good moral or strategic policy. To regularly proclaim a class of people as "abominations" is an insidious way to dehumanize and demonize.

Even the "respectable" social conservatives have chimed in, comparing gays to kleptomaniacs and alcoholics—mentally deranged folks who need help for their own good. Snipers who murder abortion providers are people they can sort of understand. Although a few conservatives have

> *"When conditions were right, entire nations have been incited by incendiary speech to exterminate whole categories of their fellow humans—for one reason or another."*

weakly condemned clinic terrorism, the overall reaction has been silence. They should, instead, offer constructive tactics that will lead to the need for fewer abortions.

If religious groups were to begin a campaign focusing on the sin of gluttony by spotlighting fat people, boycotting them from TV sitcoms, jeering at them, dehumanizing them, and demanding that companies take away their health insurance, it probably wouldn't be long before the death tolls for fat people began to rise.

Truth Is the First Casualty

Conservatives were incensed about the ads in the New York Senate race that helped defeat incumbent Alfonse D'Amato by portraying him as a supporter of clinic bombings because he voted on First Amendment grounds against a protection act that increased clinic security. Democratic political analyst Dick Morris responded that the anti-D'Amato ads were merely the flip side of tactics used by the anti-abortion movement to smear anyone who had reservations about banning late-term abortions. Gubernatorial candidate Christine Todd Whitman of New Jersey was portrayed by conservatives as a fan of late-term abortions because she wanted an exemption added to protect the mother's health. Other candidates were treated similarly.

In litmus-test politics and holy wars, truth is the first casualty. More effective than government force and political scare tactics are methods that convince, educate, and persuade. If social conservatives continue on their present course—condemning people as "abominations" and "baby killers" and the like—they will continue to be condemned as big-government zealots who generate violence and hatred.

Religious Conservatives Do Not Promote Hate and Violence

by Mark Tooley

About the author: *Mark Tooley is a researcher at the Institute on Religion and Democracy in Washington, D.C.*

Americans at 350 different locations participated in "Stop the Hate Day" on October 7, 1999, the first anniversary of the murder of the young homosexual, Matthew Shepard, who was killed in Laramie, Wyoming. Organized by the left-leaning Interfaith Alliance and Fellowship of Reconciliation, the protest was supposedly aimed at simple hate and violence.

Over 100 organizations endorsed "Stop the Hate," but oddly, none of them was conservative. Indeed, none of them could really be called anything but left of center. Many could even be called far left. Has America really become so poisonous that only left-wing groups can summon the courage to condemn criminal assaults aimed at minority groups?

Stigmatizing the Conservative

In truth, "Stop the Hate" was about considerably more than opposition to hatred. It was a not very deeply disguised effort to stigmatize conservative and traditional religious beliefs as the torpid spawning waters of prejudice and violence. Religious left groups comprised the majority of the anti-hate coalition. Apparently unwilling to engage in the specifics of a thoughtful debate, they instead resort to smearing their ideological opponents as allies of white supremacists, misogynists, and "gay bashers."

The America described by the anti-hate coalition is quite an ugly one. "Profligate hatred fills the population of this nation," the Rev. Welton Gaddy of the Interfaith Alliance warned at the anti-hate press conference. "Violence inspired by that hatred is rampant in our midst."

The Rev. Steven Baines of the Equal Partners in Faith added: "Hate violence and the rise of hate groups in America are threatening to deteriorate the very fabric of our national tapestry." Baines alleged that the killers of Matthew Shepard "had learned from society and places of worship to hate someone who was perceived to be gay."

The killers of young Shepard were bar lizards, not altar boys. Their apparent objection to Shepard's homosexuality, if in fact that was their motive, was not likely based on anything they overheard in a church. They obviously were ignorant of, or indifferent to, basic Christian teachings about human decency, as found in the Sermon on the Mount and the Ten Commandments. Yet the anti-hate coalition discerns that traditional Christian (and Jewish) opposition to homosexual practice was somehow the root cause of Shepard's murder. In their view, talk about biblical sexual morality is inherently "hate talk."

"Disagreement with the concept of sex as merely recreation is hardly evidence of hatred, much less violent intentions."

"Those who would use the Bible or Koran or Bhagavad-Gita [Hindu scriptures] as weapons of hate commit a grave injustice against our sacred traditions," said Rabbi Adat Shalom at the anti-hate press conference.

Baines said that he and his anti-hate colleagues are standing by, "needle in hand," to begin mending our tattered national tapestry and restoring it to "its original beauty."

Thanks, but no thanks. Baines' group is focused on pressuring churches to liberalize their traditional teachings that restrict sexuality to heterosexual marriage. The "original beauty" of our country is not so much the goal for Baines as creating a new egalitarian, sexual utopia where only consent determines when sex is appropriate.

Disagreement with the concept of sex as merely recreation is hardly evidence of hatred, much less violent intentions. Yet a resource booklet distributed at the press conference linked neo-Nazis and skinheads with opposition to homosexuality and a "deeply held bias" toward keeping Christianity culturally dominant in America. I suspect most Nazis and skinheads would themselves be surprised about their supposed alliance with Christian culture.

Only Politically Correct Victims Are Memorialized

Although most of the organizers of the "Stop the Hate Day" are affiliated with nominally Christian institutions, the victims they mention are only those targeted by racists and homophobes, such as Matthew Shepard and James Byrd, the black man dragged to death in Texas in 1998. Isaiah Shoels of Columbine High School is mentioned because he was targeted by his killers in April 1999 as a black student. Unmentioned are students who died professing their faith in God. The anti-Christian blasphemies shouted by the killer at Wedgewood Baptist Church in Fort Worth in September 1999 are also ignored.

Don't expect a "Stop the Hate" day at next year's anniversary of the Wedgewood murders. And don't expect participation by the anti-hate coalition in the November 1999 International Day of Prayer for the Persecuted Church, which commemorates Christians who are imprisoned or murdered in places like Sudan, China, and Saudi Arabia. This overseas persecution is government sanctioned, unlike the despicable but isolated hate crimes that occur in this country.

We perhaps should not be surprised when church groups like Pax Christi, the Episcopal Church, the National Council of Churches, Church Women United, the National Coalition of American Nuns, and the United Methodist Board of Church and Society endorse "Stop the Hate" day, along with the Gay & Lesbian Alliance Against Defamation; Parents, Families, and Friends of Lesbians and Gays; and the Religious Coalition for Reproductive Choice. But it is still disappointing.

This anti-hate coalition gives the appearance of concern only for politically correct victims, and is preoccupied with the mainstreaming of homosexuality. Without evidence, it faults conservatives and traditional religious people for creating a rampant climate of hate. And it ignores the still basic decency of most Americans, nearly none of whom sympathize with authentic hate groups. The "Stop the Hate" coalition should be more honest about its real goals.

Prison Gangs Promote Hate and Violence

by Eric Tischler

About the author: *Eric Tischler is associate editor of* Corrections Today, *a monthly journal for correctional officers.*

While the debate over corrections' role in rehabilitation vs. punishment rages on, one thing is certain: Prisons are supposed to help put a stop to crime. However, the presence of prison gangs casts the feasibility of even this modest measure of success into doubt. A popular euphemism for prison gangs is Security Threat Groups (STGs), and that term is accurate; the threat to security that these groups pose is very real. *California Correctional News* notes that "if anyone could organize the various black gangs, they would overrun the prisons and jails." From drug trafficking in the institutions to inciting riots to murder, STGs pose a threat to correctional institutions.

Cory Godwin, correctional program administrator for the Florida Department of Corrections, warns readers that if there are gangs operating in a prison, they probably are maintaining the gangs' activities on the outside. If gang members in prison can control their members outside the facility, then what are they doing when they leave the facility? And what impact are these gangs having on other inmates?

A particularly disturbing aspect of many STGs is their propensity for racial intolerance. Many gangs, especially white supremacist groups, embrace racism as a tenet of membership. According to Jack Levin, author of *Hate Crimes: The Rising Tide of Bigotry and Bloodshed,* "If you look at the prison riots over the past 10 years, you will see that the majority of them pit one group against another, for example, whites against blacks or Latinos against blacks." In other words, amid the melee, there's a racial agenda. While this causes enough problems in prison, it raises two questions: Are prison gangs indoctrinating inmates into racist schools of thought, and what are these inmates doing upon release?

The recent and dramatic death of James Byrd Jr. in Jasper, Texas, gives these

Reprinted from "Can Tolerance Be Taught?" by Eric Tischler, *Corrections Today,* August 1999. Reprinted with permission from the American Correctional Association, Lanham, MD.

questions some credence. Byrd died at the hands of James William King, a man who, prior to first entering prison, had no known history as a bigot. By the end of his sentence, King was covered in tattoos that suggested affiliation with white supremacist gangs. Upon his subsequent release, King went on to kill Byrd for no apparent reason other than the color of his skin. Did King's time in prison turn him into a killer? And, if so, how do we prevent such tragedies from recurring? While the certainty of such conversions is unconfirmed, the threat of it surely exists and it's up to the correctional industry to determine how to neutralize it.

Gang Enlistment

Perhaps the biggest obstacle to minimizing gang membership is that membership isn't necessarily just for confirmed racists. According to Brian Levin, civil rights attorney and assistant professor at California State University, San Bernardino, "There are various pragmatic reasons why a nonracist would join a racist organization in prison." Given that prison is a hostile environment, it makes sense that new inmates will need support and protection. A gang can offer just that. However, more specifically, inmates need safeguarding against other inmates who will target them because of their race and, again, the gangs will happily provide that protection.

"The prison subculture is such that there's almost this need to join up in racial groupings," says Godwin. Jack Levin further explains, "There are many inmates who feel that they almost have to join prison gangs in order to feel secure in the midst of this pervasive racial tension." The racial tension is already present between the prison gangs when a new inmate arrives. Frank Meeink, a former skinhead, confirms this.

At age 17, Meeink served a year in Shawnee Correctional Center in Illinois. He was the leader of a white supremacist gang in Shawnee, and agrees that race is an issue as soon as someone enters prison. "Once you're in there," he says, "the color of your skin is a huge part of where you're gonna sit or when you're gonna work out."

Thrust into a new, menacing environment, offenders must sink or swim, regardless of their own personal beliefs. For this reason, Reginald Wilkinson, director of the Ohio Department of Rehabilitation and Correction, goes so far as to say that, in prison, even violent crimes against members of another race aren't necessarily moti-

> *"A particularly disturbing aspect of many [prison gangs] is their propensity for racial intolerance."*

vated by racism. "With gangs," he explains, "it's sometimes hard to tell because you can't draw the line between what they're ordered to do and what they would do; that behavior may be racist or it may appear to be racist." In other words, if it means someone's survival, the commission of a violent crime against someone of another race is just part of getting by in prison; it's nothing personal.

Sam Buentello, assistant director of the STG Management Office of the Texas Department of Criminal Justice, has two different theories about racially motivated crimes in prison. First, he doesn't believe that most inmates come in with open minds and leave prison as racists. "I think a lot of them have beliefs before they come into the system and have them strengthened," he says. Second, "I do think that some people have no experience with other racial groups before they come in, but that they develop stereotypes when some groups come after them and they're in for 10 years." It makes sense that

> *"[Prisoners'] primary, initial motivation [to join prison gangs] may be protection, but the ultimate outcome is to reinforce hatred."*

someone persecuted by people from an identifiably different group might develop some specific anti-social tendencies after a while.

Brian Levin offers a logical perspective on prison racism, too. "People with a predisposition toward criminality may very well have a predisposition toward bigotry as well," he says. "They tend to be undereducated and impulsive, and cling to negative stereotypes," perfect characteristics for a racist in the making.

Jack Levin believes that, "their primary, initial motivation [to join] may be protection, but the ultimate outcome is to reinforce hatred." He says that this is especially true of offenders who have been incarcerated because of hate crimes.

While Meeink agrees that few gangs are completely race-neutral, he also believes that most people have existing racist views and that gangs help them cultivate those beliefs. "There really are no gangs that are neutral," he says. "They're always with the same people in the same cell blocks, the same cliques. I was already a skinhead when I went in there."

In Prison

When Meeink arrived in prison, he was almost immediately put in charge of a chapter of the Aryan Brotherhood. This happened, not because, at age 17, it was obvious that a kid from Philadelphia was the perfect leader for a group that consisted largely of rural bikers quite a bit older than he was. It happened because Meeink's history as a racist with a cable television show was known to members of the gang. Once he entered prison, the gang ensured that he had a venue for his hatred.

Brian Levin describes prison as a hothouse for racism. "The problems of bigotry are reinforced because prison is a closed system in which there often are no countervailing forces, such as family, church or gainful employment to discourage such activity or beliefs," he says. Once an inmate is in a gang, the circuit closes.

Some white supremacist groups have prison outreach groups. As with traditional ministries, these groups send materials to inmates. Inmates are a captive audience and, with so little stimuli, it's not surprising that they study the propaganda so thoroughly. "I find that they begin to study and do research and almost consume themselves with a lot of the literature," says Godwin. "I do find that inmates tend to become literally infatuated, and I would assume that would have a dramatic impact on feeding the flames of hatred." Indeed, some groups that proselytize hatred do so under the banner of specific religions, such as the Asatru religion, to which King apparently belonged. This devout study can have serious consequences both in and out of prison.

Uncaged Heat

The typical hate crime offender is a first-time offender, or "a teen-ager who goes out Saturday night looking for someone to bash," says Jack Levin. He estimates that no more than 5 percent of hate crimes are committed by organized hate groups, but that these groups are most likely to be involved in the most serious crimes, such as homicide. "I call these missions hate crimes," says Levin, "because the perpetrators collectively believe, or have come to believe, that they're ridding the world of evil." He says it's the support of the gang that enables these offenders to commit their crimes. "Because they've received the group's support, these guys believe they're doing something useful or positive."

Initially, being in prison didn't slow Meeink down, either. "When I got out of prison," he says, "I thought I was gonna get my cable TV show back. It was another year or so after release that I had a feeling I was wrong and another year after that to say I was wrong." It took a couple years but, ultimately, he said it.

Head 'Em Off at the Pass

If inmates are motivated to join gangs regardless of their views on race relations, how can membership be discouraged? After all, anyone and everyone is a pretty big pool of candidates. Brian Levin recommends that prisons implement anger management programs, education and encourage meaningful contact between inmates from different ethnic and racial groups.

> *"Inmates are a captive audience, and, with so little stimuli, it's not surprising that they study the [white supremacist] propaganda so thoroughly."*

Meeink agrees. He eventually was able to overcome serious indoctrination in the world of white supremacy just by playing sports with inmates of other races. He suggests that prisons offer "programs where they get people from all different races or all the different gang members and try to make mock businesses where all these guys have to work together and they get something if they achieve their goals." Working together with inmates of other races would give inmates another perspective. The repercussions could be profound. Meeink thinks such an experience would serve inmates well upon release. "When they're not in the [prison] setting any more," he says, "they're always gonna remember each other." Those memories can be related to acquaintances who haven't had such constructive contact with others.

From a preventive point of view, there is much that can be done. Godwin says Florida's response "has been directly tied to their [inmates'] disruptive behavior; it's behavior-driven," he says. "We do a threat assessment that details their disruption rates as compared to the regular population." Levin suggests "dealing harshly with gang activities and transferring leadership [of gangs]" to other facilities. The state of Ohio agrees. "We do not allow anyone to practice gang activities," says Wilkinson. "I think we do a pretty good job of discouraging it. Consequently, we don't have much problem with gang-related activities." And, just as the gangs have two-way communication between prison and the outside, Wilkinson recommends the same for corrections and law enforcement. "The other thing we do is maintain good relationships with law enforcement officials," he says. "As long as we have good intelligence about who belongs to street gangs, I think that will minimize the possibility of overt gang activities taking place in prisons."

Ohio is working on a gang renunciation program in which gang members can renounce their memberships by going through a 12-step program. "It may require special housing or transfer to another prison," he says, adding, "A big part of it is them taking a chance, taking a stand for themselves."

Ultimately, inmates do have to make the choice for themselves, but corrections professionals can help, be it by scrutinizing STGs or encouraging constructive activities that include all inmates. Meeink says he learned in prison that "what goes around comes around, and when I started trying to be positive and put out positive things, I got positive things back." That's a lesson corrections can teach its inmates.

Bibliography

Books

Richard L. Abel
Speaking Respect, Respecting Speech. Chicago: University of Chicago Press, 1998.

Donald Altschiller
Hate Crimes: A Reference Handbook. Santa Barbara, CA: ABC-CLIO, 1999.

Howard L. Bushart, John R. Craig, and Myra Barnes
Soldiers of God: White Supremacists and Their Holy War for America. New York: Kensington, 1998.

Jessie Daniels
White Lies: Race, Class, Gender, and Sexuality in White Supremacist Discourse. New York: Routledge, 1997.

Richard Delgado and Jean Stefancic
Must We Defend Nazis? Hate Speech, Pornography, and the New First Amendment. New York: New York University Press, 1997.

Betty A. Dobratz and Stephanie L. Shanks-Meile
"White Power, White Pride!" The White Separatist Movement in the United States. New York: Twayne, 1997.

Abby L. Ferber
White Man Falling: Race, Gender, and White Supremacy. Lanham, MD: Rowman & Littlefield, 1998.

Milton Heumann and Thomas W. Church, eds.
Hate Speech on Campus: Cases, Case Studies, and Commentary. Boston: Northeastern University Press, 1997.

James B. Jacobs and Kimberly Potter
Hate Crimes: Criminal Law and Identity Politics. New York: Oxford University Press, 1998.

Alex Kotlowitz
The Other Side of the River: A Story of Two Towns, a Death, and America's Dilemma. New York: Doubleday, 1998.

Gara LaMarche
Speech and Equality: Do We Really Have to Choose? New York: New York University Press, 1996.

Philip Lamy
Millennium Rage: Survivalists, White Supremacists, and the Doomsday Prophecy. New York: Plenum, 1996.

Hate Crimes

Frederick M. Lawrence	*Punishing Hate: Bias Crimes Under American Law.* Cambridge, MA: Harvard University Press, 1999.
Laurence R. Marcus	*Fighting Words: The Politics of Hateful Speech.* Westport, CT: Praeger, 1996.
Howard Pinderhughes	*Race in the Hood: Conflict and Violence Among Urban Youth.* Minneapolis: University of Minnesota Press, 1997.
William H. Schmaltz	*Hate: George Lincoln Rockwell and the American Nazi Party.* Washington, DC: Brassey's, 1999.
Timothy C. Shiell	*Campus Hate Speech on Trial.* Lawrence: University Press of Kansas, 1998.
Steven H. Shiffrin	*Dissent, Injustice, and the Meanings of America.* Princeton, NJ: Princeton University Press, 1999.
Philippa Strum	*When the Nazis Came to Skokie: Freedom for Speech We Hate.* Lawrence: University Press of Kansas, 1999.
James Weinstein	*Hate Speech, Pornography, and the Radical Attack on Free Speech Doctrine.* Boulder, CO: Westview, 1999.
Rita Kirk Whillock and David Slayden, eds.	*Hate Speech.* Thousand Oaks, CA: Sage, 1995.

Periodicals

Pam Belluck	"A White Separatist Group Seeks a New Kind of Recruit," *New York Times*, July 7, 1999.
Michael Berryhill	"Prisoner's Dilemma," *New Republic*, December 27, 1999.
Robert O. Blanchard	"The 'Hate State' Myth," *Reason*, May 1999.
Jamie Byrd	"Hate Kills," *Seventeen*, June 1999.
Christopher Caldwell	"A Fish Called Darwin," *Weekly Standard*, June 22, 1998. Available from 1211 Avenue of the Americas, New York, NY 10036.
Christian Century	"Brutal Bigotry," November 4, 1998.
Christian Century	"Violent Priesthood," September 8–15, 1999.
Christianity Today	"Who Killed Matthew Shepard?" December 7, 1998.
John Cloud	"Is Hate on the Rise?" *Time*, July 19, 1999.
Midge Decter	"Crimes du Jour," *National Review*, September 13, 1999.
Morris Dees	"Hate Crimes," *Vital Speeches of the Day*, February 1, 2000.
Richard Dooling	"Punish Crime, Not Hate," *Wall Street Journal*, July 20, 1998.

Bibliography

Samuel Francis	"Politics of Hate Crimes," *New American*, August 31, 1998. Available from 770 Westhill Blvd., Appleton, WI 54914.
Bob Herbert	"Staring at Hatred," *New York Times*, February 28, 1999.
Andy Humm	"Social Insecurity," *Social Policy*, Fall 1998.
John Kifner and Jo Thomas	"Singular Difficulty in Stopping Terrorism," *New York Times*, January 18, 1998.
Alan Charles Kors	"Cracking the Speech Code," *Reason*, July 1999.
Robert W. Lee	"Hate Crimes and Victims," *New American*, November 23, 1998.
Brendan Lemon	"The State of Hate," *Advocate*, April 13, 1999.
John Leo	"Oh No, Canada!" *U.S. News & World Report*, June 14, 1999.
John Leo	"Punishing Hate Crimes," *U.S. News & World Report*, October 26, 1998.
Art Levine	"The Strange Case of Faked Hate Crimes," *U.S. News & World Report*, November 3, 1997.
Michel Marriott	"Rising Tide: Sites Born of Hate," *New York Times*, March 18, 1999.
National Review	"Hating Crime," May 3, 1999.
Aryeh Neier	"Clear and Present Danger," *Index on Censorship*, January/February 1998.
New Republic	"The Hate Debate," November 2, 1998.
New York Times	"The Hateful Agenda of Ignorance," August 15, 1999.
David L. Ostendorf	"Countering Hatred," *Christian Century*, September 8–15, 1999.
John O'Sullivan	"Black and Blue," *National Review*, April 19, 1999.
Ursula Owen	"The Speech That Kills," *Index on Censorship*, January/February 1998.
Katha Pollit	"Hate Crimes Legislation," *Nation*, November 29, 1999.
Dennis Prager	"Anti-Semitism in America," *Wall Street Journal*, August 25, 1999.
Maria Purdy	"Hate Crime Horror Stories," *'Teen*, March 2000.
Carl Quintanilla and Kevin Helliker	"The Perils of Crying 'Hate Crime' Surface in Indian Country," *Wall Street Journal*, August 27, 1999.
Frank Rich	"The Family Research Charade," *New York Times*, December 5, 1998.
Frank Rich	"Family Values Stalkers," *New York Times*, January 13, 1999.
Jared Sandberg	"Spinning a Web of Hate," *Newsweek*, July 19, 1999.
Joni Scott	"From Hate Rhetoric to Hate Crime: A Link Acknowledged Too Late," *Humanist*, January/February 1999.
Greg Steinmetz	"German Skinhead Tells Court, 'I Am a Racist,' as Neo-Nazis Spread," *Wall Street Journal*, August 3, 1998.

Hate Crimes

Andrew Sullivan   "The 'Hate Crime' Chimera," *Wilson Quarterly*, Winter 2000.

Jo Thomas   "How an Honor Student Became a White Warrior," *New York Times*, December 12, 1999.

Daniel E. Troy   "Hate Crime Laws Make Some More Equal than Others," *Wall Street Journal*, October 19, 1998.

James Q. Wilson   "Hate and Punishment," *National Review*, September 13, 1999.

Organizations to Contact

The editors have compiled the following list of organizations concerned with the issues debated in this book. The descriptions are derived from materials provided by the organizations. All have publications or information available for interested readers. The list was compiled on the date of publication of the present volume; the information provided here may change. Be aware that many organizations take several weeks or longer to respond to inquiries, so allow as much time as possible.

American Civil Liberties Union (ACLU)
132 W. 43rd St., New York, NY 10036
(212) 944-9800 • fax: (212) 869-9065
e-mail: aclu@aclu.org • website: www.aclu.org

The ACLU is a national organization that works to defend Americans' civil rights guaranteed in the U.S. Constitution. The ACLU publishes the semiannual newsletter Civil Liberties Alert as well as the briefing papers "Hate Speech on Campus" and "Racial Justice."

Anti-Defamation League (ADL)
823 United Nations Plaza, New York, NY 10017
(212) 490-2525
website: www.adl.org

The ADL is an international organization that fights prejudice and extremism. It collects, organizes, and distributes information about anti-Semitism, hate crimes, bigotry, and racism, and also monitors hate groups and extremists on the Internet. Among its many publications are the reports *Explosion of Hate: The Growing Danger of the National Alliance, Danger: Extremism—The Major Vehicles and Voices on America's Far Right Fringe*, and *Hate on the World Wide Web.*

Aryan Nations
Church of Jesus Christ Christian, PO Box 362, Hayden Lake, ID 83835
e-mail: aryannhq@nidlink.com • website: www.nidlink.com/~aryanvic

Aryan Nations promotes racial purity and believes that whites are persecuted by Jews and blacks. It publishes the *Aryan Nations Newsletter* and pamphlets such as *New World Order in North America, Aryan Warriors Stand*, and *Know Your Enemies.*

Canadian Centre on Racism and Prejudice
Box 505, Station Desjardins, Montreal, Quebec H5B 1B6 Canada
(514) 727-2936

Affiliated with the Center for Democratic Renewal in Atlanta, Georgia, the Canadian center monitors the activities of white supremacist groups and the development of the far right in Canada. It publishes the bimonthly newsletter *Bulletin.*

Center for Democratic Renewal
PO Box 50469, Atlanta, GA 30302
(404) 221-0025 • fax: (404) 221-0045
e-mail: cdr@igc.apc.org • website: www.publiceye.org/pra/cdr

Formerly known as the National Anti-Klan Network, this nonprofit organization monitors hate group activity and white supremacist activity in America and opposes bias-motivated violence. It publishes the bimonthly *Monitor* magazine, the report *The Fourth Wave: A Continuing Conspiracy to Burn Black Churches*, and the book *When Hate Groups Come to Town*.

Euro-American Alliance
PO Box 2-1776, Milwaukee, WI 53221
(414) 423-0565

This organization opposes racial mixing and advocates self-segregation for whites. It publishes a number of pamphlets, including *Who Hates Whom?* and *Who We Really Are*.

HateWatch
PO Box 380151, Cambridge, MA 02238-0151
(617) 876-3796
e-mail: info@hatewatch.org • website: www.hatewatch.org

HateWatch is a web-based organization that monitors hate group activity on the Internet. Its website features information on hate groups and civil rights organizations and their activities.

Human Rights and Race Relations Centre
120 Eglinton Dr. East, Suite 500, Toronto, ON M4P 1E2 Canada
(416) 481-7793

The center is a charitable organization that opposes all types of discrimination. Its goal is to develop a society free of racism, in which each ethnic group respects the rights of other groups. It recognizes individuals and institutions that excel in the promotion of race relations or work for the elimination of discrimination. The center publishes the weekly newspaper *New Canada*.

League for Human Rights of B'nai B'rith Canada
15 Hove St., Downsview, ON M3H 4Y8 Canada
(416) 633-6227

Affiliated with the U.S. Anti-Defamation League, this organization works to end the defamation of Jews and to ensure fair treatment for all Canadian citizens. It publishes the annual *Review of Anti-Semitism in Canada*.

National Alliance
PO Box 90, Hillsboro, WV 24946
(304) 653-4600
website: www.natvan.com

The alliance believes that the white race is superior to all other races in intelligence, ability, and creativity. It argues that it is the obligation of all whites to fight for the creation of a white nation that is free of non-Aryan influence. It publishes the newsletter *Free Speech* and the magazine *National Vanguard*.

National Association for the Advancement of Colored People (NAACP)
4805 Mt. Hope Dr., Baltimore, MD 21215-3297
(410) 358-8900 • fax: (410) 486-9255 • information hot line: (410) 521-4939
website: www.naacp.org

The NAACP is the oldest and largest civil rights organization in the United States. Its principal objective is to ensure the political, educational, social, and economic equality of minorities. It publishes the magazine *Crisis* ten times a year as well as a variety of newsletters, books, and pamphlets.

National Coalition Against Censorship
275 Seventh Ave., New York, NY 10001
(212) 807-6222 • fax: (212) 807-6245
e-mail: ncac@ncac.org • website: www.ncac.org

The coalition represents more than forty national organizations that work to prevent suppression of free speech and the press. It publishes the quarterly *Censorship News*.

National Gay and Lesbian Task Force (NGLTF)
2320 17th St. NW, Washington, DC 20009-2702
(202) 332-6483 • fax: (202) 332-0207
e-mail: ngltf@ngltf.org • website: www.ngltf.org

NGLTF is a civil rights organization that fights bigotry and violence against gays and lesbians. It sponsors conferences and organizes local groups to promote civil rights legislation for gays and lesbians. It publishes the monthly *Eye on Equality* column and distributes reports, fact sheets, and bibliographies on antigay violence.

People for the American Way Foundation
2000 M St. NW, Suite 400, Washington, DC 20036
e-mail: pfaw@pfaw.org • website: www.pfaw.org

People for the American Way Foundation opposes the political agenda of the religious right. Through public education, lobbying, and legal advocacy, the foundation works to defend equal rights. The foundation publishes *Hostile Climate*, a report detailing intolerant incidents directed against gays and lesbians, and organizes the Students Talk About Race (STAR) program, which trains college students to lead high school discussions on intergroup relations.

Southern Poverty Law Center (SPLC)
PO Box 2087, Montgomery, AL 36102
(205) 264-0286
website: www.splcenter.org

The center litigates civil cases to protect the rights of poor people, particularly when those rights are threatened by white supremacist groups. The affiliated Klanwatch Project and the Militia Task Force collect data on white supremacist groups and militias and promote the adoption and enforcement by states of antiparamilitary training laws. The center publishes the monthly *Klanwatch Intelligence Report*, and the reports *Responding to Hate at School*, and *Ten Ways to Fight Hate*.

Stormfront
PO Box 6637, West Palm Beach, FL 33405
(561) 833-0030 • fax: (561) 820-0051
e-mail: comments@stormfront.org • website: www.stormfront.org

Stormfront is dedicated to preserving "white western culture, ideals, and freedom of speech." It serves as a resource for white political and social action groups. It publishes the weekly newsletter Stormwatch, and its website contains articles and position papers such as *White Nationalism: Key Concepts* and *Equality: Man's Most Dangerous Myth*.

White Aryan Resistance (WAR)
PO Box 65, Fallbrook, CA 92088
(760) 723-8996 • hotline: (800) 923-1813
e-mail: warmetzger@funtv.com • website: www.resist.com

WAR believes the white race is in danger of extinction and advocates for a separatist state for whites only. It publishes the monthly newspaper *WAR*, produces the *Race and*

Reason television show, distributes "white power" music recordings, and maintains a racial news and information hotline.

World Church of the Creator (WCOTC)
P.O. Box 2002, East Peoria, IL 61611
(309) 699-0135 • hotline: (309) 699-0135
e-mail: PMHale1@aol.com • website: www.creator.org

WCOTC is a religion that is based on love for the white race above all others. Its goal is to ensure the expansion, and advancement of the white race and believes that nature's highest law requires each species to fight for its own survival. It publishes *Nature's Eternal Religion*, *The White Man's Bible*, and the monthly publication *The Struggle*.

Index